What's the Point?

The Enneagram of Life

© 2002 Justin E. Tomasino Jr. Ph.D. Inga W. Tomasino

Foreword

The Enneagram leads us home from the vastness of our heart, the clarity of our mind, and the groundness of our belly. We start not even knowing the sadness of the loss of ourselves, stumbling through our lives like a person half-asleep wandering in a fog. The Enneagram is like a trumpet, cutting through the fog, beckoning us to follow its call to a place that we don't even remember leaving. The call feels somehow strangely familiar, somehow nostalgic, somehow magical. Heeding its call, we begin to witness The Mystery.
Jim Zamiska

Both as individuals and as a society, we tend to repeat the same unfulfilling patterns...over and over and over again. Scan a history book—or review your own life history as objectively as you can—and you'll see that this is true. If we just keep making the same mistakes, what's the point of it all? Why can't we change our lives so that we experience more joy, more love, and more fulfillment?

Most of us certainly have tried. Whether you've been drawn to alternative therapies and New Age interests or to the more traditional route of counseling, support groups, and self-help books, you probably feel that you're still pretty much in the same place you were when you started. The answer, however, cannot be found by *doing*—the answer lies in *understanding*.

"How," you may ask, "can I achieve true understanding?" It does not require years of therapy, attending a weekend seminar, or even doing exercises from a book. Simply *recognizing and accepting yourself for who you are*, as you are, will enable you to experience the joy, love, and fulfillment that is your birthright.

But simple isn't always easy. In early childhood most of us developed a belief that we were lacking in some way that we weren't good enough to deserve love for just being ourselves. We lost our sense of connection with Source. To compensate, we developed behavior patterns and defense mechanisms to protect ourselves and gain love and approval. The Enneagram, an ancient system of personality typing, is a valuable tool to help us identify our patterns and understand why we do what we do.

In **What's the Point?** we use the Enneagram (along with the insights and knowledge we've acquired in more than ten years of working with this system and over twenty five years working with psychology) to assist you in achieving self-understanding and self-acceptance.

The road to joyful living is a choice we all make and a road we travel with everyone else even though the journey may seem lonely at times.

The Enneagram liberates by freeing one from judgment toward others. Rather than seeing another as being odd or annoying, they are seen as possessing unique individual traits that are just another color in the rainbow of life. On the other hand, it is easier to understand why the personal chemistry between oneself and another works so magnificently. The result is that it is much easier to be harmonious with one's friends and genuinely interested in those with whom one has less in common.

The Enneagram opens the door to the truth that we are one.

Tom Benson

Acknowledgments

We wish to thank our editor, Anet Paulina; Teresa Kassube for her cover graphics; Jim Zamiska for introducing Justin to the Enneagram in 1991; fellow school teacher, Tom Benson; Dr. Margaret Summers, Principal The Pinnacle Charter School, who gave Justin the opportunity to make a difference; the International Enneagram Association for keeping the Enneagram alive; all of the Lightworkers in the world who are working for awakening and consciousness; our children; and our families and friends who put up with our preaching.

Introduction

For thousands of years, we have been killing each other in the name of our deities—to protect ourselves, to dominate others, and to accumulate resources. Arab and Jew, Catholic and Protestant, and Serb, Slav, and Croat continue to slaughter each other. Why? The justifications vary: Each side will justify its cause with logic such as "An eye for an eye," "God is on our side," or "We don't want their kind here."

Despite centuries of civilization and progress, little has changed, because we have continued to think, treat others, and do things the same way we always have. Continuing in our old behaviors and expecting different results is a sign of insanity.

But there is a way out, which is outlined in this book. It may be so foreign to you that as you read it, you may need to open your mind, suspend your beliefs, and allow yourself the opportunity to expand into new realms.

This is necessary because beliefs are limited to belief structures and then cemented in us as truths. Yet truths that change or truths that have opposing truths are not real truths at all; they are not absolute. And unless truth is absolute, it is only a manifestation of the ego; it is not a reality. Absolute truth does exist, but at deeper levels.

Ego is a survival mechanism of every living organism. It helps us to cope with fear. It is the mechanism that keeps us from running into traffic or walking on railroad tracks in front of trains. When activated in the body, it triggers the hypothalamic

region and produces adrenaline that activates either
fight or flight mechanisms. Contrary to popular
opinion, there is nothing wrong with ego. The
problem occurs when ego is out of balance, putting
the body in a constant frightened state. Rather than
the ego being there to serve us, we exist to serve the
ego.

As you read this book, you may find yourself
offended, or even angry. Try to discover the source of
your anger, for anger is resistance to reality,
generated from distortions of truth. The ego creates
these distortions to make us think we are separate
from everyone and everything else, a "truth"
supported by the five senses. Our physical senses—
smell, hearing, taste, touch, and sight—are limited.
For example, we know that dogs hear beyond our
range of hearing and eagles see beyond our range of
sight. If we know that our senses are limited, we
must assume that our perceptions viewed through
these senses are limited. We have other senses that
we were born with and learned to deny, thus these
senses were not developed. These senses lie within
the spiritual world and are accessed through pure
feeling. Most of us, however, learned to turn off our
feelings, and that is when we got into trouble. We
thought that the only way to work through the world
was with our rational minds that are controlled by
our five physical senses.

Thinking that we are separate allows us to
justify violence against others, which creates victims
and perpetrators—what we call victim consciousness.
This is a duality because victims need perpetrators

and perpetrators need victims. One cannot exist without the other.

Victim consciousness is in turn used to justify revenge: Victims get even by becoming perpetrators themselves. They become what they have judged, tried, and convicted. This condemnation of others and ourselves remains in our psyches, surfacing as guilt or shame. This cycle goes on and on and will perpetuate itself until something happens to disrupt it.

This book suggests returning to the loving selves we were born as, because it is only through love that we can evolve into beings of love. Our biggest block or challenge is to recognize the truth of reality, the cause or root of our behaviors.

The Enneagram, as we will introduce it in this book, is an effective tool that, when used properly, will assist us in our way of communicating not only with ourselves but also with others. When we can understand others and ourselves better, we can open ourselves to living a more joyous life with greater consciousness.

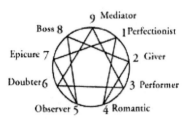

History of the Enneagram:

It is uncertain where the Enneagram had its beginning. It is believed that it first started over two thousand years ago with a group of Eastern mystical practioners called Sufis, who used it in what they called the Oral Tradition. The Oral Tradition was used so that the deepest truths discovered through the Enneagram were passed along verbally by masters of the technology.

Gurdjieff learned the Enneagram in Armenia from the Sufis and brought it to Russia, where he taught it for many years. From there it made its way to Chile via Oscar Ichazo, who further developed it by linking the symbol of the Enneagram (a nine-pointed star) to the nine passions—the seven deadly sins plus deceit and fear. Claudio Naranjo brought the Enneagram to the United States in the early 1970s. He is known for linking the Enneagram to psychiatry.

Besides the Enneagram looking like a nine-pointed star, you will see three parts representing three divine laws. The circle around the Enneagram represents a universal Mandela or the unbroken circle, oneness, and unity. The triangle represents the trinity that is used in many of the world's religions. The third part is the star itself, which (as explained later in the book) shows how, over time, all the energies of the different points flow into each other.

The Nine Enneatypes

There are nine basic Enneagram personality types called Enneatypes. No one type is better or worse than another type. The nine types signify nine basic ways of perceiving the universe. It is like having a camera that represents the universe. If you took pictures of the same point in space using nine different lenses, you would see nine different ways of viewing the same thing.

When going through the Enneatypes (nine personalities of the Enneagram) it will be a challenge not to see yourself in all of the types. It may be easy to box yourself into a type before you have looked at all the types. Therefore, we have included several levels of personality identification to help you identify or "fine-tune" the mirror. These you will recognize under the headings of subtypes: Instinctual and Centers, Hornevian Groups (based upon the research of Karen Horney), and moving toward Wings (the Enneatypes on either side of the main type). One type will resonate most with you.

Each of these types has three subtypes, thus there are twenty-seven subtypes. In addition to the subtypes, there are energy flows toward the Wings of each type, which are adjacent to the main type. For example, an Enneatype Four may move toward either the Three or the Five, exhibiting traits of those types along with his own.

The Enneagram is not a system that puts people into boxes and then tries to define who they are. Rather, it is a system that identifies the boxes we put ourselves into and explains behavior categorized in those boxes. Since there are over six billion people on the earth, there are over six billion personality variations. We will not discuss these 6 billion variations in this book. Below, we describe each Enneatype in a summary form. Later in the book, each type is described in detail.

One: The Perfectionist – Type Ones feel they have to be good little boys or girls. They know what is right and wrong and will gladly tell you. Ones live in relative perfectionism. They are detailed and picky, and may be moralistic and preachy.

Two: The Giver – Type Twos need to be needed by others. They are always looking for ways to help other people, even if the others do not want the help. Twos may flatter to get attention. They can be seductive if that's what it takes to get to help someone.

Three: The Performer – Type Threes are hard working and achievement-oriented—the classic "Type A" personality.. They are motivated and competitive. Threes are image conscious and feel they must look good at whatever they do.

Four: The Romantic – Type Fours are quite artistic and moody. They are the drama kings/queens of the Enneagram. Fours like to live life at its highs and lows; every other way is mundane to them. They want to be seen as special and unique.

Five: The Observer – Type Fives are disengaged in life and live life in their heads. They seek knowledge, and to obtain knowledge, Fives are willing to give up the finer things in life.

Six: The Doubter – Type Sixes are the cynics, the doubters. They question everything and trust is difficult for them to achieve. Sixes look for security and safety, and need to be part of groups of belief systems.

Seven: The Epicure – Type Sevens are always planning. Fun loving, they are constantly on the go seeking new experiences. Sevens experience life through superficial lenses, and do not delve too deeply into anything.

Eight: The Boss – Type Eights are the bad boys/bad girls of the Enneagram. They are very assertive and get their way through intimidation and power. Eights look for protection and in doing so, they push their energies outward to keep their distance from people.

Nine: The Mediator – Type Nines need peace and harmony in their lives, and will sacrifice themselves in order to achieve it. Nines are easygoing, affable people. They see both sides of the story and can help others through problems.

Fixation Points on the Enneagram

It is important to note that each of us is unique and special. We choose our own fixations and it does not matter what the fixation is, it is still a fixation. For example, what difference does it make if we fixate on envy, anger, greed, lust, vanity, pride, gluttony, fear, or sloth? It is like choosing the poison that will kill us. The more fixated we are, the more our natural internal energy flow is blocked. During stressful times, we tend to fixate towards the outer ring of the Enneagram and exhibit highly dysfunctional behavior.

If we do not clear the real cause of the fixation, we may move toward what is called the path of disintegration. The path of disintegration occurs when the pain is so great and the defense mechanisms associated with the Enneatype are not working. We then move backward along the arrows contained in the Enneagram energy flows. For example, as an Eight fixates on lust and exhibits passionate behavior like vengeance, he may find that his senses engaged in the environment become overwhelmed. He may move toward the Five, where he will withdraw to lick his wounds and plan strategies to exact further vengeance on his perceived enemies.

The I AM Center of the Enneagram

As we clear the causes of the dysfunctional behavior, we fixate less and move back toward the I AM center of the Enneagram. At the center, we achieve balance and natural energy flow. There, we exhibit virtuous behavior. We feel joyous. We understand profound concepts of forgiveness, compassion, and purpose. We exhibit more of the virtuous traits of all the Enneatypes.

Through choice, we develop traits of personality. Ego is developed from personality as a defense mechanism to cope in the world. Personality, or some say ego, filters (buffers) outer world stimuli and processes reality in different ways. It is important to note the difference between personality and ego as used in this book. Ego is a part of personality. It is our fight or flight mechanism—our survival system—and is used by our bodies to protect us in times of trauma. The problem is not with ego per se; it is that ego is out of balance—it is in charge and making decisions for us. Naturally, the ego should serve the personality, not the other way around.

When we observe our behavior and find it dysfunctional, we tend to alter the behavior rather than seeking its cause. This is a trick of ego that makes us think the behavior is the problem. We call this fixing the symptom and not embracing its cause. Identifying symptoms may help us find the cause of the problem. However, symptoms may reveal other symptoms and not the real causes. If you were to visit a dentist with a painful toothache and the dentist gave you a shot of Novocain and sent you home, he relieved the symptom of the pain temporarily but did not seek the underlying cause of the pain. It is when the dentist identifies the cause of the pain and treats it that the pain will disappear forever. It is when we seek and see the truth in our pain that we will cure it forever.

The Ego

The ego lies to us and tells us never to be satisfied with who we are. Instead, it keeps us anxiously seeking to be better, because our current self is not good enough. This is a fixed core belief, the belief that we are not good enough to be ourselves without condition. In truth, we are already the best we can be in the present moment. It is in the present moment that truth arises. In each moment there exists universal perfection and purpose. We may not see perfection and purpose in each moment, but it is not important that we see them. What is important is that we know they exist.

Using the Enneagram, we see the lies the ego tells us that identify how we think we are not good enough in the current moment. Here are examples of what the ego might say for each of the nine types:

One: The Perfectionist – "When I am perfect, I will be loved, and I will be good enough."

Two: The Giver – "When others need me, I will be loved, and I will be good enough."

Three: The Performer – "When I accomplish all I need to accomplish, I will be successful and loved, and then I will be good enough."

Four: The Romantic – "When I am seen as unique, someone will rescue me; then I will be loved, and I will be good enough."

Five: The Observer – "When I know enough, then I will be loved, and I will be good enough."

Six: The Doubter – "I will be secure when the world around me is secure; then I will be loved, and I will be good enough."

Seven: The Epicure – "When I experience everything, I will be happy and then I will be loved, and I will be good enough."

Eight: The Boss – "When I am strong and in control, I will be loved, and I will good enough."

Nine: The Mediator – "When there is peace and harmony, I will be loved, and I will be good enough."

It is helpful for us to remember that we are more than our personalities; we are beyond that. We are a portion of the divine, the Creator, but we have fallen asleep. Our essence is spirit, and within that spirit lies our soul. When we become less identified with our ego, it becomes less important to us. That is when we take on our real identity, which is our true nature.

The purpose of the Enneagram is not to help us get rid of personality. When we get in touch with our deepest selves, we do not lose our personality. It becomes more transparent and flexible and helps us live our lives, rather than taking over our lives. As we become less identified with personality, it becomes a smaller part of who we are. There is more intelligence, sensitivity, and presence underlying it that uses the personality as a vehicle rather than being driven by it. We actually find our identity as we move towards our essence.

The Structure of this Book

This book is organized into three parts:

Part I: Our Dysfunctional World, explains our dysfunctional behavior, or rather our symptoms of behavior. How we view love with conditions and how we think we are separate from everything, when we are really all connected.

In Chapter One, we delve into depth explaining the differences between love and fear. Judgment is a prime concept to understand because when we judge others, we are judging ourselves. What disturbs us in other people is a mirror of what most disturbs us in ourselves.

Chapter Two examines duality and how it skews our view of reality. We explain in detail how our perceptions are limited by our five physical senses. Observers view the world without understanding how they affect what they are observing, but there can be no observers without the observed. We delve into how each of us projects our unconscious needs onto the environment and that what is returned to us is a mirror of what we project.

Chapter Three explains the process of ego development and how the ego got out of balance and took control of us. We introduce the Enneagram and begin to build it into the system used for healing.

Part II: The Enneagram: A Tool for Diagnosis, describes the Enneagram and the breakdown of each personality type—the Enneatypes. We explore how each Enneatype behaves and the consequences (or cause and effect) of the choices we make. We will help you find your identity within the system.

Chapter Four explains how we lose our balance and look externally for what we cannot find internally. This process develops unconscious desires for those things we really have inside that we believe are not there. We describe the triads of the Enneagram: Instinctual, Feeling, and Thinking. The Hornevian Groups (Assertives, Compliants, and Withdrawns) are examined as well.

Chapter Five describes the importance of energy movement through the Enneagram and how energy movement promotes health. We identify the fixations and passions of each Enneatype and how these affect each type. The Heart Point and Stress Point of each Enneatype in introduced and examined. We explain the Thinking, Feeling, and Doing Centers of each Enneatype and their importance to growth.

Chapters Six through Fourteen examine each Enneatype in detail. We list specific areas including basic needs, basic fears, mottos, speech patterns, and projected mirrors.

Part III: Making Our Way Back, will give us a roadmap back to whom we really are and how we can achieve this with compassion and forgiveness.

Chapter Fifteen describes the nature of communication and how important communication is to understanding. Each Enneatype is described by the method used to communicate in the world. This chapter aids us in identifying Enneatypes by noticing a person's speech patterns and demeanor.

Chapter Sixteen examines intimacy and its importance in relating to other people and ourselves. We describe how each Enneatype creates its own intimacy patterns, as well as each type's positive and negative patterns.

Chapter Seventeen introduces the tool called forgiveness. We list the traits necessary to see beyond our five physical senses to achieve real forgiveness. We describe what real forgiveness truly means, and how each Enneatype can achieve real forgiveness rather than pseudo forgiveness. Each of us loses, gives away, or has taken from us spiritual values that we need to live in forgiveness. These values are described in this chapter.

Chapter Eighteen provides the next tool toward enlightenment: compassion. Compassion requires a higher level of understanding than most of us currently use. We list the truths of compassion and how each of these truths relates to each Enneatype. Here, we link those values that were lost, taken, or given away and how they relate to compassion. Each Enneatype and its compassion truth are described. We show how we can use compassion for better understanding of other people and ourselves.

Chapter Nineteen explains what consciousness and enlightenment are and how we can wake up from our deep sleep to live these gifts. Enlightenment is available to all of us in every moment. When we wake up to its glory, we achieve it without effort. We list the traits necessary to awaken and describe the process necessary to live in joy.

These techniques are simple, yet difficult to achieve as long as we cling to fixed core beliefs that limit our possibilities. Only when we release our beliefs and allow truth to arise can we journey into ourselves and see ourselves for who we really are—warm loving beings, each containing gifts endowed to us through the Creator.

Justin E. Tomasino Jr., PhD
Inga W. Tomasino

Part I: Our Dysfunctional World

As with all truths . . . they belong to the Universe.
Inga W. Tomasino

1 Fear vs. Love

L ove is allowing someone to be who they are and accepting them just the way they are. We must remember that we are on different journeys in life and get to choose our own paths. Love is the only reality that exists; everything else is an illusion. Love is the glue that holds the entire universe together.

Who are we to judge anyone's path? Who are we to judge our own path? We learned fear, comparison, and judgment. When we judge others, we judge ourselves, because we compare others to our values and our morals, holding them up to our standards. Judgment is based on right and wrong. These, as other dualities, are relative to the judge. What we judge in others as wrong, we judge in ourselves as something relative to our perceptions of right and wrong, and vice versa. What we fear in other people is reflected by what we fear in ourselves. Other people mirror us, so that we may see who we are. What we mirror or project outside ourselves are those things that were lost, taken, or given away. This manifests as fear because we fail to see the perfection in ourselves, and thus we fail to see the perfection in others.

The Nature of Fear

Fear keeps us from seeing who we really are. There is but one fear: the fear of being who we really are. This fear is manifested as the fear of not being good enough and (as a possible result of truly being yourself) the fear of abandonment. Without the fear of being who we really are, we become self-actualized, which is our normal state of being.

It is difficult to be oneself when from the day we are born, our parents try to make us into someone else rather than accepting us for who we really are and encouraging us to be ourselves. The result is rejection from those who "love" us. This rejection makes an imprint upon our personalities and creates the fear that stays with us all of our lives until we do something to reverse it.

Some of us may say that our problems existed in previous lives and current suffering was from a past life—that we are only paying the karma from these past lives. However, if we did exist in previous incarnations, wouldn't the grace of God allow us to live this moment cleanly? If not, and we truly do choose to carry over something from previous incarnations, what we carry over is energy that we choose to cling to. In the current incarnation, we would create energy patterns similar to those we created in past lives, patterns that would bring forth the lesson or whatever we are trying to harmonize. Since energy patterns are most important, what occurred in previous incarnations does not matter because the same energy is in the now.

Cosmic karma is the force of creation. It is part of the whole, the unity of existence. Our ego makes us believe that our problems are associated with a different time, and thus implies that we are stuck in our suffering because we are paying off some karmic debt. As long as we choose to cling to these lies, we are stuck in the suffering, but we do not have to be stuck there. The *Bhagavad Gita* says, "All karma, or effects of actions, completely melts away from the liberated being who, free from attachments, with his mind enveloped in wisdom, performs the true spiritual fire rite." As long as we think we are separate from everything else, we delude ourselves into thinking we are the "doer" and the center of the universe. This is selfish and narcissistic. Freeing ourselves from the fetters of karma allows us to experience life without filters.

Until we see the fear for what it really is, it presents itself in the present as something that bothers us in other people and is reflected back to us. We react to external stimuli with feelings from the past. When faced with a painful situation, ask yourself if you have ever felt that way before, and be honest with yourself. The details of the current situation do not matter. What matters is the energy of the feeling. If you can answer yes, then a past event is driving your perception of the present, thus distorting current reality.

Recurring Energy Patterns

Situations have a way of repeating themselves in the recurrence of energy patterns to help you learn the truth. Have you seen patterns develop in your life that seem to repeat over and over again, and you do not know why you always get into the same situations?

Our souls put us into these situations until we learn from them, break the patterns, and move on to other truths. Until we learn from the past, we become victims, continually repeating these energy patterns. When we feel energy arise from within ourselves, even if it is negative energy, it is a natural process to recognize the truth in the energy. Truth is like cream and oil: in the long run, it rises to the top. This is so because energy in the universe is freely flowing. When we choose to hold on to energy due to some type of hurt, the energy always tries to free itself, but cannot do so until we understand the truth about it.

The Meaning of Real Love

Love means to allow ourselves to be ourselves and accept it. If there is something about us that we do not like, we can change it. It is easier to change the way we perceive others than it is to change them. Many of us go into relationships expecting to change our partners with the hope that, "He [or she] will see it my way" or "If you love me, you will do...[whatever.]" If they love you, they will accept you for who you are. Anything else is conditional, and thus, not love. Since the definition of love disallows conditions, then real love is unconditional.

Conditions make love a transaction. This is similar to giving. If we give to receive, we are not really giving. We are transacting, like a business deal.

If we give love with the expectation of receiving love in return, we are neither loving nor giving. The paradox is that when we truly love and give without an expectation of something in return, love returns to us. It is automatic and always fills the void.

Some of us confuse love with lust. When our sexual drive is sparked by someone we meet, it is not love. It is our primal physical desire to mate, to propagate the species. This is not to say that this desire is not real or should be repressed. Our bodies tell us many things; this is one of them. The sexual desire for someone could be a result of love for that person, but it is not love in itself.

The Nature of Anxiety

Some of us confuse love with anxiety we developed at a young age and relate love to this anxiety. If we perceive love to be the anxiety we received from a father who was cold and challenging, we may align ourselves with people who are like this and think it is love. In truth, it is just a desire to connect with someone who reminds us of what we think love is. If we had an overbearing mother and associate this trait with love, we may think someone who is overbearing is showing us love, so we search for that type of person. The overbearing person dictates our every move, tells us what to do, and appears to be concerned about us. However, there are really two things going on in this example.

First, the overbearing person feels the need to be overbearing, but doesn't recognize this trait in himself. His obsessive desire to dominate may be due to associating love with dominance or with its antithesis, submissiveness.

Second, the submissive person has linked love to submission, but doesn't know it. This may be a workable arrangement for a relationship, but is it love? The dominator is never happy with the dominated because he is constantly trying to change her to fit his standards, since he perceives her standards as not good enough. The dominated person may resent the dominator, but if she thinks his behavior shows love, she submits, just like she did as a child. She may submit without resentment and try to change the dominator as she tried (or wanted to try) to change her relationship with one of her parents. This behavior is obsessive, but the person exhibiting the behavior doesn't know it.

Unfulfilled Needs

When we are born, we have all the things we need. We are born as loving individuals. What happens along the way? Why do we acquire obsessions and addictions? Why can't we accept things the way they are?

The primary reasons are unfulfilled needs. As babies, we need to eat when we are hungry. We need someone to change our soiled diapers when we are wet. We need someone to pick us up and hold us when we need to be picked up and held, and to feel the warmth of the caring, loving body of our parents. Except for breathing and basic motor responses, as babies, we are helpless. We depend upon someone to provide for our needs when we need them. When we are hungry and our stomachs ache with hunger, we feel the pain and cry out. There is no other way to communicate our desires to our parents except for the cry. If our parents think it is not time for our feeding, or say, "How can he be hungry? We just fed him," they may initiate anxiety in the baby, especially after repeated episodes of this situation. As infants, we do not understand the concept of time and "the right time for feeding." When our stomachs burn, we know only the pain. This is true of other needs also. Many parents check their babies for hunger, wetness, and sickness, but ignore or don't recognize the need to be held. Many times we hear, "Don't pick him up; you'll spoil him." We spoil our children when we *don't* pick them up and hold them. Let them feel love. The words are insignificant to babies, but they recognize the feelings.

When our needs are not met, we cry out for help. When help does not arrive, we cry louder and more deeply as the pain increases, as the need is not met. Eventually we internalize the lack of response as a love void, turn off the pain, and move a step away from feeling. It is the beginning of anxiety. These first anxieties are the deepest and most difficult to transform because they began when our rational mind could not comprehend the pain and the lack of response from a loved one.

What happens as we grow from infancy to toddlers and our parents associate love with candy, television hours, performance, etc.? We hear, "If you learn to play the piano, I'll buy you a bicycle." Thus, love?

Pete experienced the throes of anxiety as he and Beth had the greatest challenge of their twelve-year marriage. He was violent and threw Beth around the bedroom, threatening to expel her from the home in the morning if she didn't promise to give up her relationship with another man. Beth called me at 3:00 a.m. and we discussed the situation. After the call, she went to Pete and helped him break through his suffering. He remembered that when he was five years old, his mother warned him and his brother and sister that their father was due home and was going to beat them. They ran into a closet and clung to each other for protection. When their father found them there, he noted that they were naked and made them feel shame. He beat them mercilessly. Pete was afraid of his father seeing the shame of his wife having an affair, triggering shameful anxieties that would result in getting beaten, so he clung to Beth. He would cling to his sister the most, because he found it made the beatings more tolerable.

Pete's memory was the reason he was feeling the way he did when he was following his father's example by acting violently. This scene was similar, however, to the end of a movie. His clinging to his brother and sister for safety was a learned response from his past—an automatic response to the fear of being beaten by his father, someone whom he believed should love him.

What event programmed him to use this defense? The program built into us as children is like a computer programming loop. Given the same input, the computer will continually play back a situation, time after time, endlessly, until someone interrupts the program with a break.

Beth had to decide whether to follow her feelings or try to turn the feelings off, continue to feel miserable in the marriage, and abandon her path.

Paths of Love or Fear

When we are presented with choices in life, as we are constantly, our decisions are sometimes a choice between a path of love or path of fear. Along the path of fear are the programmed responses we learned as children. There lie the "shoulds" and the "shouldn'ts" heard from the little voice in our head that says, "You should do this because it is the right way, " which presumes that there is a right and a wrong way. It is the way we were raised to believe what is right and wrong. Since right and wrong are dualities, each depends on the other for definition, and this duality is relative to the observer.

We don't know what is right or wrong anymore; in fact, we're not sure there *is* right and wrong. We choose the way of fear because it is the way we have struggled all our lives to "earn" the love of our parents. It is the familiar route, the one most comfortable to us. But repressing our real feelings and succumbing to our programmed responses keeps us wallowing in our misery.

A result may be jealousy or envy: We think someone has something we don't have. Where does jealousy come from? How many times as children do we watch our parents cuddle a sibling or give the sibling attention we don't receive? We yearn for the warmth and attention, but are told: "Boys don't hug," "You'll thank me when you're older," or "She's a baby and you're not anymore." However, we need warmth and reassurance from our parents as we grow, regardless of our age or gender.

Judgment

What happens when we judge people? What in them are we judging? When we judge others, we rate them by our standards. We compare them to what we know or what we would do in situations. Each of us has his own standards. The standards we have are those we have learned; some are so old we don't even know we have them or where they came from. We think these standards are facts. "Couples shouldn't live together unless they're married." "You should go to church every Sunday." "Children should be seen and not heard." "Boys shouldn't cry." "Spare the rod, spoil the child." "Nice guys finish last."

These are not facts, but they are used and quoted so often that we think they are. They are opinions. Everyone has opinions; we use them as justifications for our actions. We are not sure there are many facts in this world.

We judge others and ourselves based on these opinions, which are "shoulds" and "shouldn'ts." They are programmed responses. What would happen if we had no more "shoulds" or "shouldn'ts"?

Happiness Is Not a Goal

Did you ever meet someone whose goal in life was to be happy? Happiness is not a goal, but life itself; it is part of our journey. In "The Wizard of Oz," when Dorothy walks on the yellow brick road with her friends to achieve happiness by going home. At the end of the journey, she discovers that happiness was available to her whenever she wanted it; she just didn't know it.

At the beginning of the movie "Citizen Kane," when Charles Foster Kane dies he utters his last words: "...Rosebud." This great film is about a reporter's search to find what "rosebud" meant in Kane's life. Charles Foster Kane was a man who had everything money could buy, and hoarded all that he owned. He had everything except for what money couldn't buy—love. Although the reporter never found out what "rosebud" was the viewer sees that it was the name of the sled Kane had as a child. He used the sled to shield himself from the man who came to his Colorado home to take him from his parents to educate him and to show him the finer things in life. This was the last time Kane was happy and felt love, and was the scene he returned to as he died alone and in misery.

How many people in our society have become millionaires and are miserable? Why? Because there is something meaningful and deep that is missing in their lives: love.

How important is love? Love is the most compelling force in the universe. It is all there is. When we are caught in a love void, or anxiety, we are out of balance with the universe and thus, ourselves.

Twenty six years ago, I began a search for myself. I read all the most insightful books available at the time, most of which recommended a daily ritual of some kind to convince myself that I was happy and worth being on Earth. I wondered why this happiness and joy couldn't be automatic. Why should I have to convince myself every day? I realized that even though I performed the rituals, I still was not happy. What was keeping me from being happy? Why must I work at something I thought to be the most natural thing in life?

This is when I started my journey into my anxieties. I began to question each of my responses to external stimuli, especially those that were negative or caused my stomach to churn. I found that when I felt pain, I rarely was reacting to the present situation. The stimuli reminded me of the pain I had been repressing all my life. For example, when I was angry at a job counselor for advising me to get a haircut before an interview, I found I wasn't really angry at him. I went home and let the pain come up. After reliving a traumatic experience I had blocked from my memory for twenty three years, I knew the anger was directed at my parents, not at the counselor. The counselor was trying to help me.

What is time and space? I noticed from re-experiencing my feelings of the past, it was as though they were now. There wasn't any time interval between the traumatic event and now. I know logically that many years had passed, but within the feeling, no time had passed. I surmised that feelings are made of energy that travels at the speed of light. If Einstein was correct, there would be no time. Time is man made. If this is true, then would all that there is at a feeling level be now?

What about thought—doesn't it also travel at the speed of light? Or does it go faster? How fast is fast? If thought is like feeling, then there is no time interval for thought, and all thought occurs at once. The Bible says "the Word" came first. I wonder if it really means that thought came first, and then the Word. (However, many people speak before they think, so perhaps the description is accurate!)

If the universe has been around forever, what is the value of a human who lives 100 years? Is it as significant as a grain of sand on all the beaches, on all the worlds in the universe? Insignificant, but yet significant.

Most of us have learned that there is one God. I agree, because I feel God in everything. God is not the sun, but I feel God in the sun. God is not the earth, but I feel God in the earth. God is not the flowers and the trees and the animals, but I feel God in all these things. I am not God, but I feel God in me.

If all these things are parts of God, then who or what is God? God is all things, all that there is, was, and ever shall be. If all that there is, is together then that must be God. God is ONE, ONE God.

If God is creation, what happens when I think? Is my thought creation or am I only tapping into thought of the universe that is already there? If my thought is creation, is this the part of God in me? If I am only connecting to thought that is already there, then am I like a radio receiver, choosing thoughts like dialing in to different frequencies? Why do I think, anyway?

What is my soul? My soul or spirit is part of who I am. It is the energy that differentiates my body from being alive and being dead. My spirit is energy. This energy is light. Light is a standard in the universe. The molecules in a solid vibrate at a frequency slower than the speed of light. This makes it appear as though the mass is solid, but the space between the nucleus and the electrons in the atom that make up the molecules of the mass is substantial compared to its size. What is this space? It can't be "nothing"; I don't know what "nothing" is. Is it the same as the space between the earth and the sun, or between the sun and the other stars? We know this space is not "nothing." If nothing else, it is a conduit for light, those frequencies of light we can see and those we cannot see.

Hurt, Shame, and Envy

Fear is the reaction to the perception of lack of love. Hurt, shame, resentment, envy, and anger are some of the responsive behavior patterns of fear.

Fear is life-threatening. It is the process our minds and bodies go through when we are in a fight for our lives. The gazelle is afraid when it scampers from the lion that is in search of dinner. The mouse is afraid of the cat that pounces upon it. What happens when the baby who is dependent upon it parents screams out for food and doesn't receive it, or cries out in the night from the darkness, wanting to feel the warmth of its parents, and doesn't receive it? To the baby, is this life-threatening? Some of us may believe the infant cannot think and therefore is oblivious to the fear. "We must train him for the realities of life," we say. What does thinking have to do with the feeling of hunger or abandonment? The lamb has no thought as it hangs dying with its throat cut. It feels terror. The baby also feels terror; it has no other choice. We are correct in assuming the infant cannot rationalize the fear. All it knows is the feeling of terror.

Experiences like these are the beginning of anxiety. Anxiety is the fear of something that doesn't really exist as a life-threatening situation in the current moment. When we are infants, like these are the beginning of anxiety. When we are infants we repress the fear and start what we describe as the "tree with many branches." We root ourselves in the ground and the main branch of our lives; the trunk grows out reaching for the sky. The trunk is our path to main growth through love. When repression due to fear occurs, we create alternate paths or side branches to escape from the pain. Each time we escape from pain and travel along a different branch, we extend the length of it. Eventually we grow branches to the branches, until we have created a complex web of escape routes (no pun intended).

Compulsions and Obsessions

In our life experience as an adult, we sometimes reach a point where we react to external stimuli in an irrational, compulsive, or obsessive manner. These are the points where we skip off the main tree trunk and travel along one of our self-made branches in a time of confusion. This is an automatic response—we don't know when we are doing it. For example, suppose our spouse or companion has an affair and we find out about it. Our first reaction is that of anger or rage. We feel deeply hurt, and lash out at our companion. Our second reaction is that of internalization because we feel distrust, betrayed, cheated, abandoned, not good enough, etc. We look for the reasons the person cheated on us.

We go out on branches as our ego is searching for a way to repress the pain. Did our spouse create the pain in us? Most of us would answer with a resounding "yes," but we don't think so. By their actions, our companions remind us of a pain already inside us. This pain is what puts us onto other branches. Although we don't realize it, the feeling is the same as we have experienced before, when it was a life and death struggle for us as an infant. It is only the stimuli are different.

For an infant, one event may cause dissociation to a branch of the tree if the event is traumatic enough. More often, however, it is a long, protracted series of experiences, day after day, that creates these branches. We have found that the anxiety that leads to the main branch usually originated with a series of events (typically a lack of hugging, warmth, feeding, and other expressions of real love).

Who is responsible for this feeling—our spouse or companion? How can they be responsible for a pain that we created years ago?

Internal Programming

We are programmed much like computers. The moment we enter this world, the programming begins. We are stuck in programming loops. If this...then do that; after that, loop back to if. We do this over and over, unconsciously, until we interrupt the loop.

To interrupt the loop, we must first recognize that it is there. How can we recognize when we are in a programming loop? Usually, it is when we cannot accept people for who they really are or accept a situation for what it really is. It is when we impose our opinions on a situation or judge ourselves or another person. If someone doesn't do as we expected, we judge them using our own standards. Who are we to impose our standards on someone else? People do what they do because they do it.

There is no other meaning, but we continually put meaning on behavior. Why did your spouse have an affair? Because she did.

If you judge people, you have no time to love them. Mother Theresa

2 Duality: A Skewed View of Humanity

Who are we really? Are we our names? Are we what we believe? Are we what we eat? Are we what we drive? Are we our bodies, minds, or souls? We are all of these and more.

Quantum Analysis

Quantum physicists found that atoms contain 99.9% space. If the nucleus of an atom were the size of a grain of sand, its electron would be 20 building stories away and the size of a speck of dust. What is in between? If the quantum physicists are correct, then we are 99.9% space, as are all of our third-dimension realities. Atoms are made up of energy, and the space between nuclei and electrons is energy also. We are energy fields vibrating at different frequencies. At quantum levels, we are wave patterns of probabilities. In *The Web of Life,* Fritjof Capra writes,

> These patterns, moreover, do not represent probabilities of things, but rather probabilities of interconnections. The subatomic particles have no meaning as isolated entities but can be understood only as interconnections or correlations, among

various processes of observation and measurement.[1]

This means that there is no separation between subatomic particles and that each particle depends on another, then another, and so on. It is a unified whole, a web, a matrix. Furthermore, at the subatomic level, energy cannot be destroyed. Capra continues:

> This is how quantum physics shows that we cannot decompose the world into independently existing elementary units. As we shift our attention from macroscopic objects to atoms and subatomic particles, nature does not show us any isolated building blocks, but rather appears as a complex web of relationships among the various parts of the unified whole.[2]

Our perceptive sense organs register these fields as third-dimension realities, thus we seem to perceive this dimension as solid and real, when in fact it is not. Compare it to seeing a movie. When the movie is playing, we tend to identify with the characters, and at times, think it is reality. Awareness tells us that the movie is really actors and actresses playing roles that make us think it is real. However, the movie is only a reflection of still photographs running quickly through a projector and

---

[1] Fritjof Capra, *The Web of Life,* 30.
[2] Ibid.

shown on a screen. It is an illusion. Moviemakers, through editing and special effects, can make us believe anything. This is like life—the ultimate virtual movie.

If you are not convinced it is an illusion, think of it in another way. During the time it has taken you to read this chapter, you may think that you have not moved. You may be in a comfortable chair in your living room. However, we are on a rotating orb somewhere in space revolving around a yellow star called the sun. The Earth rotates at approximately 1,000 miles per hour or 17 miles every minute; therefore, we are at least 34 miles from the point where we were two minutes ago. This estimate does not include the distance the earth traveled during its revolution around the sun. Furthermore, the entire solar system, anchored by the sun, moves within the Milky Way galaxy, and the galaxy moves within the universe. Are we still in the same spot? It is an illusion to think so.

Universe: One Song

What holds this dimension and its perceptions together? Everything is made of exactly the same basic stuff, only in different form. What holds it together is love—or God, or the Creator. If it is all one, the name of this divinity does not matter; labeling it would only serve to limit it. The term "universe" means "one song." It is not logical to assume that one thing does not affect another. In the universal web of existence, one act affects the entire web—it is not limited to one effect for each cause.

The idea that one act causes one effect implies separation and negates unity.

Quantum physicists found that when one observes an experiment expecting it to have a particular result, the anticipated result is observed. For example, when an electron is sought as a wave, it is found as a wave rather than a particle. If it is sought as a particle, it is found as a particle rather than a wave, Electrons can be both waves and particles simultaneously. Fritjof Capra, in *The Tao of Physics,* explains:

> At the subatomic level, matter does not exist with certainty at definite places, but rather shows 'tendencies to exist,' and atomic events do not occur with certainty at definite times and in definite ways, but rather show 'tendencies to occur.' In this formalism of quantum theory, these tendencies are expressed as probabilities and are associated with mathematical quantities which take the form of waves. This is why particles can be waves at the same time.[3]

Quantum physics has shown that subatomic particles are not isolated and alone. They are connected to the whole, the unity of all. There are no gaps. Capra continues:

> Quantum theory thus reveals a basic oneness of the universe. It shows we cannot

---

[3] Fritjof Capra, *The Tao of Physics,* 68.

decompose the world into independently existing smallest units. As we penetrate into matter, nature does not show us any isolated 'basic building block,' but rather appears as a complicated web of relations between the various parts of the whole. These relations always include the observer in an essential way. [4]

The observer affects the observed because the observed changes with the energy from the observer. We learned this effect in grammar school when the school principal walked into the classroom, sat down in the back, and said, "Don't mind me; I am just observing." The dynamics of the class changed due to the presence of the principal. Observe people in conversations at parties (or elsewhere). Watch the dynamics of the energy as people enter and exit the space or enter and exit the conversation. Notice how the conversations change as someone enters into the area of the conversation. That person need not say anything; even their presence changes the dynamics. When someone else either joins or leaves, the conversation or the dynamics of the room energy will change. We need not say anything; we need not do anything. We need not be anyone beside ourselves. The only thing that is important is our presence. It is our energy (soul) that alters the dynamics of the space we occupy, and it is our soul that affects the people with whom we interface. This concept frees us

---

[4] Ibid.

by helping us realize that we need not try to be someone other than who we are.

The Human Experiment

We are spiritual beings conducting an experiment to experience humanity. Our soul is not in our body; our body is in our soul energy field. Why did we choose to experience being human? Having human experiences means that we are connected to everything else and are interdependent beings in this dimension. As interdependent beings, we are able to know ourselves through others. Other people mirror us. How would God know God-self unless the God-self was reflected back to God? So in a sense, we are God-selves reflecting our divinity back to other God-selves. Nevertheless, if all is one and this is love or God, then everything else is an illusion that we created to experience being human. The illusion is the separation from All-That-Is. This is accomplished through the ego, which makes us believe in separation.

The ego was created for the purpose of self-preservation. Unfortunately, religions teach that this separation is an original sin, thinking that the Creator was angry at our choice to separate, when we really did not separate. How can a loving Creator be angry if the Creator is experiencing the beauty and perfection of itself? A newborn baby comes into this world so pure and innocent—how can one believe this person is bad or has sinned? That is absurd.

Think of it in another way: We cannot be duplicated. We can have ourselves cloned, but the clone would have only our genetic makeup, not our experiences, our personality, or our soul. These are what make each of us unique. In our uniqueness, we are perfect. We are perfect for who we are every moment, and there is only one moment: this moment, the present, the now. If one ant were dislocated somewhere in the universe, the structure of the universe would collapse. Honor your perfection. Honor your beauty.

Since there is no real separation from All-That-Is, and our perceptions indicate there is, then it is our perceptions that create the separations or dualities. The duality of male and female energies creates the first perceived separation. The only real difference between male and female is physical, which allows procreation to occur. One gender needs the other; if either one is missing, procreation does not occur. Right/wrong, good/bad, and up/down are also dualities. Right cannot be defined without wrong. Good cannot be defined without bad. Up cannot be defined without down. They are all relative to the observer; what may be right to one may be wrong to another.

Each piece in a duality is not the opposite of the other. It is like a wave; within a wave is a crest and trough. If either the crest or trough were in itself an opposite, this would imply that either was a whole unit in itself. This is not true because if either were not present, then the wave would not exist. Rather than being an opposite, each side of a duality is in an intimate dance with the other side. When we can overcome dualities by seeing them for what they really are, we will be able to overcome the limitations of this dimension. In the Gospel of Thomas, Verse 22, Jesus said:

> *When you make the two into one, and when you make the inner like the outer and the outer like the inner, and the upper like the lower, and when you make male and female into a single one, so that the male will not be male nor the female be female, when you make eyes in place of an eye, a hand in place of a hand, a foot in place of a foot, an image in place of an image, then you will enter [the kingdom of heaven].*

Free Will

We could not experience the human plane fully without the concept of free will that allows us to choose the way we want to live our lives. This we have, and always will. How can one choose God without a free will to do so? If there were no choice, then choosing God would be fruitless because it would be our only apparent choice. What blessing would there be if we chose God and knew there was no other choice? Ultimately, at the most profound level, there is no will but God's will. All choices come down to love or fear. Since love (God) is all there is, then fear must be an illusion. So why are we so afraid? Many of us have become lost in the illusion within the illusion. We take life too seriously. We don't laugh enough; we don't have enough fun. When we were in kindergarten, most of us laughed many times throughout the day. As adults, we tend to laugh just a few times a day, if that. What happened?

We stopped taking responsibility for our own happiness, and try to make our happiness contingent upon external events. We try to give away our power to others in exchange for happiness and attempt to please everyone. This we cannot do. We are here to please ourselves, and are responsible for 100% of our choices and 100% for our happiness. Many of us do not think we are good enough to be happy; we think of ourselves as bad or flawed. If this were so, it would mean All-That-Is makes mistakes. All-That-Is does not make mistakes. When we think of ourselves as bad or flawed, these are only false beliefs we have manufactured. When we think these thoughts, and believe them, we see the badness or flaws in everyone and everything else. Thoughts attract like energy, and energy creates. If we create badness and flaws, then that is what we will get, and we will project them onto the external environment. If we think perfection and beauty, then this is what we will get, and we will start to see the perfection and beauty in everything and everyone. When you look at a tree, notice if it has any flaws—perhaps a knot, or distorted branches and leaves. Do these flaws make the tree less beautiful? Of course not—it is the flaws that make the tree special and unique. In that uniqueness is the Creator's perfection, love, and beauty. The tree has a unique purpose, and within that purpose, there is beauty and perfection...the same as in us.

Humanity Is an Illusion

Pain and suffering are part of the world of humanity, but are not of the world of divinity. We live in both worlds simultaneously. The world of humanity is the illusion. The source of pain and suffering is in our emotional and physical bodies. When we choose to listen to our emotional and physical bodies and allow the true causes of our pain and suffering to surface, we will be able to see the truth within. Then the pain and suffering will vanish, to be replaced with joy and ecstasy.

We tend to lie to ourselves about the real causes of the pain and suffering. Most of us choose to blame other people or external stimuli for the pain. Most of the time, however, it is a projection of ourselves onto something else that makes us believe the cause is external. We are seldom upset about what we think we are upset about; usually we are reacting in the present to something that occurred in the past. When we look at the patterns, we may realize that the feelings are familiar even though the event is different. This is called projecting.

Projections and Mirrors

Projecting not only occurs in the personal realm, it is also contained in the collective consciousness. For example, Saddam Hussein is hated and feared by many Americans. However, you may recall that he was our ally when he was bombing

Iran when Iran was our sworn enemy. When Iraq attacked Kuwait, we went to war to stop the tyranny of Hussein. Saddam Hussein is the man we love to hate, but remember that millions of Iraqis love him. What are the things we say we hate most about him? Here are some typical responses:

He is a liar and never keeps his promises.

He kills his own people.

He enslaves his own people.

He starts wars for personal gain (the oil fields in Kuwait).

He is developing weapons of mass destruction, such as atomic and biological weapons.

He will not allow United Nations inspectors to inspect his country for weapons of mass destruction.

He keeps secrets from the citizens of Iraq and does not give them the real story.

In the history of America, have we ever lied to other countries or failed to keep our promises? What about our promises to the Native Americans when treaties were reached? Did we tell them we would take their land because our desire to possess was stronger than theirs, and that we would kill them if they tried to defend their land? Did we tell them that we would give them unfertile land in the desert and expect them to farm it, even though they were not naturally farmers? When gold was discovered on those lands, did we move them again because of our greed? Have we ever mass murdered our own people, like the Native Americans (including the women and children)? Have we ever enslaved people on this continent? What about the Africans brought here in slave ships, the Arawaks, and the Taino? Did we cage the Japanese Americans during World War II, while the German Americans went free? Have we ever started wars for personal gain, like the Spanish American War? Do we have weapons of mass destruction, including atomic bombs and biological weapons? Would we allow Iraqis into our country to inspect our arms facilities for weapons? Do we keep secrets from our citizens and give them only partial truths, for national security reasons?

What we hate about Saddam Hussein is what we cannot reconcile in guilt and shame within ourselves. We repress these emotions, denying that they exist, while we project them onto the environment. We will continue to look for the Husseins of this world until we find a way to forgive ourselves for our own imperfections. It is the same as looking within each individual: What we find, if we search truthfully, is similar to what was discussed above. The things we judge other people for are the things we judge about ourselves.

Since hate energy attracts other hate energy, Saddam Hussein and others like him will continue to thrive. The only way to transform this energy is to forgive ourselves for what we consider wrongs and to see them for what they really are. Then we will be able to transform the hate energy into love energy.

The Answer Is: Love

Some of us may think that we will never love these types of people. As long as we think this way, we cannot shift our feelings and will be stuck in the hate energy. This is not healthy. Some people thrive on hate energy because they feel it gives them power...our power. When we are able to transform it into love energy, their purposes will disappear, and the hate energy will dissipate.

Even though we shift to a love position, we do not need to agree with someone's methods, nor is it necessary that we like them. We need to see the divineness in all situations and know that everything occurred as it was supposed to in order to advance our level of consciousness. All-That-Is does not make mistakes. We do not need to know the divine purpose of what occurred; we only need to know that there is divine purpose. At the very least, we can bless the event. We do not need to accept it, condemn it, make sense of it, or condone it.

The entire universe, including our human world, is a flow of energy—that's all it is. We take the flow of energy and allow it to move through the body. Without impediment, ego is at its ebb and self-actualization at its height. With impediment or grasping, ego is dominant, and self-actualization is minimized.

Ego and Separation

Ego is a survival mechanism of every living organism. It helps us cope with fear and keeps us from running into traffic or walking on railroad tracks in front of trains. Physiologically, ego responses affect the hypothalamus in the brain, triggering a reaction that results in the production of adrenaline, the hormone that activates either fight or flight mechanisms. Contrary to popular opinion, there is nothing wrong with ego. The problem occurs when ego is out of balance and causes the body to remain in a constant state of fear. When this happens, rather than the ego serving us, it seems we exist to serve the ego.

Who Are We Really?

It is important for us to distinguish among Essence, personality, and ego. We use the term Essence to denote the core being of all there is. It is who we really are: loving beings experiencing the universe, the universe in itself, and God. We define personality as the part of us that reflects our real self. The ego is the part of the personality that exists at the instinctual level. The ego reflects the false self or shadow self. In the Enneagram system of personalities (explained further in the next chapter), there are two ways of viewing the ego. We may use the Enneagram as a tool to explore ego fixations, obsessions, and compulsions, or use it as a tool that reflects spiritual enlightenment. The Enneagram of fixations, obsessions, and compulsions reflects ego development. In ego development, there are false core beliefs of separation from the All-That-Is. The Enneagram of spiritual enlightenment reflects essential development and virtues that lead to self-actualization. We may also use both Enneagrams to help reflect the total nature of the universe.

If self-actualization is an enlightened state in which ego is minimized, then what is left when we attain self-actualization? Do we melt into the universe? Do we lose our identity? We will still be there as self-actualized people, each of us maintaining a distinctive, unique identity within unity. For example, if we look at a Persian rug, we may see the rug in its entirety, but the rug contains distinctive patterns in it. Each pattern appears to be unique, part of the overall pattern of the rug. Nevertheless, smaller, more intricate patterns appear. This is similar to personality. Within the great pattern of the universe are personality patterns that are part of the whole pattern of unity. When we observe animal behaviors, we note that every animal has a distinct personality that is as unique and authentic as the patterns in the rug.

Ego – Out of Control

Ego imbalance develops through learned distrust in the environment. As children, we learned to perceive the environment as hostile and dangerous. The government, corporations, and our caretakers support this. We are not allowed to be ourselves and are not accepted for ourselves. We learn that we are flawed, and lose the basic instinct of love. We fall asleep, and narcotize to who we really are. The sense of losing the loving environment creates distrust in the universe; we no longer feel that everything will work out for the highest and best good if we surrender, let go, get out of the way, and develop courage to be ourselves. This distrust makes us think that we must change or control the environment in order to be safe and to experience the true love that we think is missing. We "act out" an obsession or passion to find a route to return to the loving state, and put on a "false face." We view the world through the filters of the passion or fixation we developed, hoping that someday we will be loved for who we really are. But we have fallen asleep to who we really are, and we don't even know it! Along the way we encounter false selves, not only in ourselves but in the people with whom we associate. We are afraid to be ourselves because we fear that if "they" really know who we were, they would abandon us, because we are not good enough for love. We are flawed.

The ego (sometimes called the "shadow self") makes us think we are alone, that we are separate from everything else. Ego makes us believe the world is a dangerous place. We can try to change it (aggressive), run away from it (withdraw), or give up ourselves and go along with it (compliant). The ego develops the illusory belief of separation of mind, body, and spirit, and we see the world as eventless, random, and meaningless. Ego, through the illusory belief of separation, misses the big picture. It is out of balance and experiences the world through "egoic filters": passions, obsessions, etc.

In our distrust of the environment, we doubt universal intelligence. We doubt the Creator, and doubt the existence of goodness. We are angry with the Creator, and feel betrayed because we think we were abandoned. We lack faith in the universe.

Ego fixations develop in the nine distinct ways of viewing the world. The Enneagram of Ego Fixations is a system of ego traits based on the fixations and passions that identify each of us. Although there are many variations and subtypes of the Enneagram, there are only nine basic ego fixations (covered in Chapter 3), which manifest through the means of the passions looking for love. Love is not attainable through the passions because to know love is to know the truth—and truth is not recognized by the ego. The ego-self lies to us because it wants us to stay in the state of fear, which is the survival mechanism of the ego at work. We become so familiar with the fear state that it seems normal to us. In this way, the ego controls us, and we serve it.

3 Identifying the Enneatypes

The Enneagram

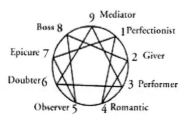

Enneagram Symbol and Personality Types

The Enneagram can be used as a tool to identify which of the nine ways of viewing the universe best describes us. When we see ourselves as we truly are, we can recognize that the passion that we have created is a first step in the journey to wholeness and self-actualization. When we know ourselves, it makes it easier to know others, and to recognize that understanding, compassion, empowerment, and forgiveness arise through love and truth. This re-enables enlightenment by cleansing all the egoic filters we have imposed upon ourselves. Enlightenment is not specific experiences; it is experiencing and understanding life and ourselves the way they really are without egoic filters. We begin to see reality objectively and to experience essence, the essence in all there is.

The Enneagram symbol is a circle that contains an equilateral triangle and a hexagon. The circle symbolizes the universal wholeness—that everything is connected and is one. The equilateral triangle symbolizes the trinity, or the spirit, heart, and body. The hexagon symbolizes the law of seven, which is about movement and development. Though the universe seems static, it is always in movement, a natural and spontaneous unfolding. The triangle and hexagon are connected and form nine points, starting at the top with the Nine personality and moving clockwise, One through Eight. The number of the personality is not important; the numbers are simply a convenient way of identifying the nine distinct ego fixations. Briefly, the Enneagram of personalities manifests fear strategies of not being good enough, with the possible result of abandonment.

Basic Characteristics of Each Enneatype

Enneatype One – The Perfectionist

- ✍✍View the world as black and white, with few shades of gray.

- ✍✍Are very conservative and resist change.

- ✍✍As children, learned to repress their emotions, which caused internal anger and rage.

- ✍✍Try to be "good little boys and girls" because they think it will bring them love and acceptance.

- ✍✍Often have impeccable grooming; may be compulsively neat and organized.

- ✍✍Tend to be critical and judgmental, both of themselves and other people.

- ✍✍Possess integrity, and hold themselves and others to high moral and ethical standards.

- ✍✍Strive for perfectionism and are detail-oriented, accurate, and precise.

✍✍Follow rules and procedures closely and expect others to do the same.

✍✍Like to "preach and teach"—enjoy correcting others' mistakes and giving advice on the right way to do things.

✍✍Professionally, they make good accountants, policy and procedure analysts, ministers, and house cleaners.

✍✍Mottos: "Practice makes perfect." "Rules are meant to be obeyed." "If it ain't broke, don't fix it."

✍✍Ego message: "When I am perfect, I will be loved, and I will be good enough."

Enneatype Two – The Giver

✍✍Strive to be needed by others, and equate this need with love.

✍✍Feel that other people need them more than they need other people, which lead to a feeling of pride.

✍✍Use flattery and service to others as a means of gaining love.

✍✍Have a high need for intimacy.

✍✍Learned to shut themselves down and do whatever was necessary to please others.

✍✍Possess the ability to please even the most difficult people.

✍✍Fear rejection and believe that rejection equals worthlessness.

✍✍Use manipulation to get attention, and exceed other people's boundaries in an effort to meet others' needs.

✍✍Tailor behavior to suit each person they interact with, and may have a sense of many "false selves."

✍✍Prefer to stay in the background promoting others; are attracted to people on their way up socially.

✍✍Professionally, they do well in service professions such as doctor, nurse, counselor, and nun.

✍✍Mottos: "A friend in need is a friend indeed."
"What would people do without me?"
"How can I help?"

✍✍Ego message: "When others need me, I will be loved, and I will be good enough."

Enneatype Three – The Performer

✍✍The typical hard driving, achievement-oriented, Type A personality.

✍✍The American corporate ideal and classic "workaholic": life is centered around work, accomplishments, and success.

✍✍In childhood, they were valued for their accomplishments

✍✍Strong sense of vanity—they have a burning desire to succeed and to look good in doing so.

✍✍Value personal achievement above all else, and equate failure with rejection, unworthiness, and shame.

✍✍Extremely image-conscious—they can change their image at will to obtain the most approval.

✍✍Charismatic and self-promoting in areas where image and presentation are important

≤≤Proficient at networking; prefer to associate with people who can help them achieve career objectives.

≤≤Tend to avoid deep, intimate relationships.

≤≤Can be "smoke and mirrors" types who deceive people into thinking they really care.

≤≤Are impatient with the natural unfolding and energy flow of the universe; want to make things happen within their own timeframes.

≤≤Professionally, they make a good salespeople, advertising executives, chief executive officers, and performers.

≤≤Mottos: "My work is never done." "Fake it until you make it." "Appearances are everything."

≤≤Ego message: "When I accomplish all I need to accomplish, I will be successful and loved, and then I will be good enough."

Enneatype Four: The Romantic

≤≤Want to be seen as significant, different, and unique.

✍✍In childhood, felt abandoned by parents and siblings and withdrew from other people.

✍✍Withdraw into an inner world of romantics fantasies, preferring it to real life.

✍✍Envy others who seem to have the happiness they lack.

✍✍Prone to dramatic emotional displays—may be "drama kings and queens."

✍✍May have a victim mentality and want sympathy from others.

✍✍Look outward for love and strive for relationships to fill deep emotional holes.

✍✍Crave dramatic relationships—prefer emotional highs and lows, and get bored with ordinariness.

✍✍Want to be rescued, but may push away a person who wants to rescue them.

✍✍Highly imaginative and creative; may excel at music, art, writing, or any area where introspection and fantasy are important.

✍✍Professionally, can make good graphic artists, sculptors, musicians, and writers.

✍✍Mottos: "No one understands me."
"How can people be so happy—my world is falling apart!"
"Romeo, Romeo, wherefore art thou, Romeo?"

✍✍Ego message: "When I am seen as unique, someone will rescue me, and then I will be loved, and I will be good enough."

Enneatype Five: The Observer

✍✍Strive for competency through the accumulation of knowledge.

✍✍Their greatest fear is of being incompetent, useless, or incapable.

✍✍In childhood, withdrew into a cerebral world to feel safe and avoid painful emotions.

✍✍Analytical and logical; avoid acting until they feel they have enough information.

✍✍Love to theorize and analyze, and spend a lot of time and energy thinking.

✍✍Tend to be observers in life, thinking that the observer has no effect on what is being observed.

✍✍Have difficulty with intimacy because they want to avoid painful emotions.

✍✍Handle spontaneous reactions in social settings awkwardly because they need time to reflect and figure things out.

✍✍Usually are on the cutting edge of technology and have the latest gadgets for storing and retrieving data (computers, personal digital assistants, etc.).

✍✍Seek to become an expert at something, even if the subject is obscure and has little relevance to the real world.

✍✍Professionally, they make good technical analysts, accountants, teachers, and ministers, and excel in areas that allow them to work on their own.

✍✍Mottos: "Knowledge is power." "Geniuses are rarely recognized in their own time." "First you buy books; if any money is left over, you buy food."

✍✍Ego message: "When I know enough, then I will be loved, and I will be good enough."

Enneatype Six: The Doubter

✍✍Strive for security by being part of a group or belief system.

✍✍In childhood, learned that the environment was not safe, and constantly anticipate danger.

✍✍Doubt their own thoughts and decisions, which lead to procrastination.

✍✍Are drawn to external means of feeling safe, such as joining corporations, the military, churches, or political groups.

✍✍Tend to align themselves blindly—when loyal to causes and belief systems, they dislike it when others question these beliefs.

✍✍Are team players and can be counted on to do their part.

✍✍They question authority and tend to be skeptical.

✍✍Have many successes, but concentrate more on their failures.

✍✍Project their fears onto the outside world, looking for someone to blame.

✍✍When stressed, find it difficult to remain still.

✍✍Professionally, they make good inspectors and quality assurance specialists, and excel at jobs that require troubleshooting, asking probing questions, and looking for inconsistencies.

✍✍Mottos: "Be careful out there." "Whatever can go wrong, will go wrong." "Why me?"

✍✍Ego message" "I will be secure when the world around me is secure, and then I will be loved, and I will be good enough."

Enneatype Seven: The Epicure

✍✍Strive for happiness externally, through superficial experiences.

✍✍Are incessant planners but continually change their plans, trying to cram in as many activities and events as possible.

✍✍Intensely dislike being bored, and over-schedule themselves to ensure that they always have something interesting to do.

✍✍Fear and avoid intimacy because it requires commitment and depth, which they view as limiting, boring, and possibly painful.

✍✍Have many superficial interests, experiences, and friendships, but prefer not to delve deeply into anything.

✍✍Prefer to be involved in the high-energy beginning and planning stages of relationships and activities, and become bored with the lesser energy stages.

✍✍Are quite charming, personable, and fun to be with.

✍✍Love spontaneity and enjoy events and experiences that involve high energy levels,

✍✍Feel entitled to what they want from life, and tend to pursue it without much regard for others.

✍✍In romantic relationships, prefer open-ended agreements rather than marriage.

✍✍Professionally, they do well in public relations positions, and excel in jobs that require little detail and offer a wide variety of experiences.

✍✍Mottos: "Variety is the spice of life." "Life is too short not to have fun." "You only live once—if you don't enjoy it, it's your own fault."

✍✍Ego message: "When I experience everything, I will be happy; then I will be loved, and I will be good enough."

Enneatype Eight: The Boss

✍✍Strive to protect themselves through control of the environment, by pushing against it and being strong.

✍✍Are direct, forceful, and aggressive—can be bullies.

✍✍Are impulsive and often act before thinking.

✍✍Tend to pursue what they want in a lustful manner.

✍✍Have "all or nothing" attitudes— something (or someone) is either right or wrong, good or bad, strong or weak, useful or useless, etcetera.

✍✍Like to make the rules and expect other people to abide by their rules.

✍✍Attempt to control possessions, territory, and people, and are protective of their significant relationships.

✍✍Are very productive and accomplish a great deal, especially in the business world.

✍✍Love debates and confrontations, and will stay awake at night thinking of ways to make a point.

✍✍Prefer to be given a summary or the bottom line—usually don't want to be bothered with the details.

✍✍Professionally, they make good leaders, managers, and defense attorneys, and excel in areas where major changes need to be made.

✍✍Mottos: "Only the strong survive." "My way or the highway!" "I am the great and powerful Oz!"

✍✍Ego message: "When I am strong and in control, then I will be loved, and I will be good enough."

Enneatype Nine: The Mediator

✍✍Strive for peace and harmony in both their internal and external environments.

✍✍Are easygoing, friendly, and approachable.

✍✍Strongly dislike conflict and anger, both within themselves and in other people.

✍✍Find it difficult to make decisions and set priorities because they see everything as equal.

✍✍Indecision leads them to look externally for help, usually from friends, family, and other significant relationships.

✍✍Have difficulty saying no, and often agree to things they really don't want to do in order to keep the peace.

✍✍Look for other people with whom to merge their lives—those who will provide them with direction and support.

✍✍May withdraw into an inner world of fantasy, which numbs them to the real world.

✍✍Tend to become overwhelmed by things they have to do; may choose to do nothing and numb themselves further.

✍✍Are open-minded and able to see all sides of the story, which gives them great skill in mediating and helping others through problems.

✍✍Professionally, they make good therapists, mediators, ministers, and referees, and excel in areas where they feel they are needed.

✍✍Mottos: "Easy does it."
"Peace at any price."
"I don't really care—let's do it your way."

✍✍Ego message: "When there is peace and harmony, I will be loved, and I will be good enough."

Effectiveness of the Ego Strategies

For all the Enneatypes, none of these strategies for returning to love and trying to be "good enough" works, because it is the ego that makes us think we need to strive to attain love. In truth, love is all there is, and it exists in the present moment at all times. If we really needed to strive to attain love, then love would be conditional, based on some type of performance or change in oneself. Love is unconditional, so any thought, feeling, or action associated with striving for love is a fear-based, egoic concept.

Ironically, none of the actions, thoughts, or feelings noted in the Enneatype descriptions above will help the person realize the desired goal. For example, the Three will never accomplish everything, the Five will never attain enough knowledge, the Six will never feel safe and secure in the world, and the Seven will never experience everything (especially at deep, meaningful levels). The obsessive actions or non-actions taken by each Enneatype in an effort to have love result in alienating them further from real love. For example, in striving for strength and control, Eights bully others, creating rage and resentment for their tactics. Nines, in seeking peace and harmony, do so at their own expense by flat-lining their responses to life experiences, which causes them to withdraw even further.

Part II: The Enneagram: A Tool for Evaluation

4 A Balancing Act

Water seeks its own level. This is the principle behind a siphon, and the cycle in nature that allows all things return to their source. Rain eventually returns to the ocean.

To live in the present, we must remain on the border between calcification and chaos. Living in the past is calcification; living in the future is chaos. There is but one moment in which to live: the now, the eternal now.

Humans seek balance in two ways, internally and externally. When the balance achieved internally shifts as we grow, the external balance also shifts. Internal balance is always achieved before external balance. Although it may seem that everyone is seeking external balance, it is reached only after internal balance is achieved. If one area of self is out of balance, the other areas of self-attempt to compensate, and sometimes the results are disastrous.

Internal balancing includes both vertical and horizontal integration. Vertical integration comprises the balancing of body (instinctual), mind (thinking), and spirit (feeling or heart). Horizontal integration includes balancing of masculine and feminine energies, and left and right brain hemispheres. All the parts are interconnected and act as an entirety, with a oneness, as a flow of energy. When the self is out of balance, it seems to split and separate, and access to other areas becomes difficult or repressed. This illusory division of self may cause obsessions, compulsions, phobias, neurosis, or psychosis.

Internal: Vertical Integration

The hypothalamic region of the brain is the ancient "reptilian" brain that controls the instincts and contains the primitive nervous system. Its primary function is to regulate vital functions such as breathing, heartbeat and blood flow, digestive and urinary processes, and hormonal output. It attempts to keep all these functions in balance or homeostasis. The hypothalamic region is present before birth and fully functional at birth. Fortunately, because of this system we do not have to regulate our bodily functions with conscious thought.

The Body:

Our bodies are amazing machines. We incarnate into them to experience being human, which means being fully feeling, thoughtful, and active. Our bodies must be properly nourished with a balanced diet of proteins, fats, carbohydrates, vitamins, and minerals in sufficient quantities. Lack of these will result in disease. English sailors learned that the lack of Vitamin C caused scurvy, so they started bringing citrus fruits (rich in Vitamin C) on their journeys, earning the nickname, "Limeys."

Our bodies change with age, which necessitates changes in eating habits. For example, Justin had gum surgery several years ago. Although at the time he was primarily vegetarian, after the surgery he dreamed of prime rib and baked potato. Throughout the next day, he craved prime rib and baked potato. That evening, although chewing was difficult, he listened to his body and ate what he craved. His body was telling him what he needed to heal properly. Our bodies do not lie to us; they always let us know what they need for healing and maintaining proper balance.

Because our bodies are organic machines, they need time to rest, which means that proper sleep and relaxation are necessary to maintain balance. Sleep patterns vary from person to person, and within each of us they vary at different times. When we are ill, for example, we usually need additional sleep. Sleep allows us time to heal and to rebuild our bodies. The *Bhagavad Gita* says, "Oversleep dulls the nervous system; too little sleep produces a tendency to sleep against one's own will."

Our bodies need regular patterns of eating, relaxing, working (exercise), sleeping, excreting, and waking. Irregular schedules result in hunger, irritability, tension, stress, constipation, and exhaustion.

The Mind:

The intellectual or cortical region of the brain is the area that forms ideas and thoughts, rationalizes, and provides meaning to experiences. With thoughts, we can control impulses and emotions that arise from the other two systems. The cortical region, also known as the neo-cortex, begins to develop at approximately age six and continues to grow until about age twenty. The neo-cortex is the seat of the ego, the area where we learn to stay away from lions, porcupines, and skunks. We also learn where to find food and how to grow it. The neo-cortex is the level that calculates; it is mathematical and logical. Time associates at this level.

Our mind is very powerful—so powerful that it is the only part of the trilogy of body, mind, and spirit that will lie to us. Thoughts create energy, and energy attracts like energy. If our thoughts are aberrant, the energy created is aberrant. If our thoughts are loving, the energy created is loving.

Aberrant energy affects our bodies, as does positive, loving energy. Think about times you've had thoughts of guilt, worry, resentment, vengeance, greed, hate, or envy. What was the state of your body? You probably produced tension in the shoulders or throat, "butterflies" in the stomach, a headache, or lower abdominal pain. You may have developed cold sores. The times we recall when loving thoughts were present—times when people we are close to told us how much they love us, we received a gift for no particular reason, or were recognized for the beautiful person we really are— were times we felt connected to Unity. We were blissful, painless, and joyful.

Aberrant thinking reduces the effectiveness of our immune systems. The way we think is vital to the health of our bodies— studies consistently show that optimists are healthier (and live longer) than pessimists. The egoic system is the seat of fear. Fear creates aberrant thinking—fear of being ourselves that manifests as fear of not being good enough, with a possible result of abandonment. Fear affects the body's chemistry and balance. Psychiatric drugs often are prescribed to correct chemical imbalances that cause insomnia, depression, anxiety, and other fear-related symptoms. The selective serotonin reuptake inhibitor drugs (Prozac, Paxil, and Zoloft) help relieve these symptoms by increasing the availability of the neurotransmitter serotonin. Low levels of serotonin activity in the brain have been linked to suicide, violence, and aggressive behavior.

The Spirit:

The brain's limbic system processes our emotional responses. It is the seat of our feelings, the area that is active when we enjoy art, music, poetry, and dreams. Though this system is present at birth, it does not begin activity until we are about six months old, and it continues to mature as we age.

Our spirit knows the oneness of all. The biggest difference between spirit and mind is that in the mind there are beliefs; in the spirit there is knowingness. When the spirit is out of balance, repressed, in the self, we are oblivious to our true nature. The *Bhagavad Gita* states, "So long as a human being lives [in] ignorance of his true nature, only his body and egotistical mind have reality for him; his soul is as though eclipsed."

Our spirit vibrates at the highest vibratory frequency of self. When spirit lowers its frequency and condenses, it creates mind and body. Everything is energy vibrating at different frequencies; regardless of the frequency, it is all Creator.

Methods for achieving balance with spirit include prayer, meditation, and chakra balancing. Prayer is asking for assistance from the divinity within; meditation is listening to the inner voice for solutions. Chakras are areas in the body where energy vibrates at specific frequencies in harmony with spirit. There are seven major chakra points in the human body. Chakras may be balanced with tones, colors, aromatherapy, or hands-on energy alignment practices such as Reiki.

Internal: Horizontal Integration

The brain weighs about three pounds, is the size of a grapefruit, and has the consistency of a ripe avocado. From the top, the brain looks like two halves of a walnut (hence the term –"walnut brain"). These are the left and right hemispheres. We need the brain's management functions to breathe, metabolize food, excrete wastes, and set our heartbeat. The brain regulates all voluntary and involuntary movements, sensory impressions, emotions, creativity, thinking, and personality. Unlike a computer, the brain can tell the body to relax, daydream, laugh, become inspired, experience consciousness, perceive meaning, and fall in love.

We have both masculine and feminine sides; these are aligned with the left and right brain hemispheres. Essentially, the left-brain, masculine side is logical, linear, organized, factual, and sequential. The right brain, feminine side is creative, circular, global, and assigns meanings to events.

We live both in the world of spirit and the world of humanity; the left-brain is in the world of humanity and the right brain is in the world of spirit. The left-brain is time-oriented and the right brain is timeless. Everything we do takes both sides of the brain to function; otherwise, nothing gets done. There is a constant flow of information energy from one side to the other. For example, the left-brain tells us it is time to balance the checkbook. It knows we need a calculator, bank statement, and pencil. It must reconcile the numbers to the penny, and is willing to spend as much time as necessary to achieve this goal. The right brain feels it is not necessary to be accurate to the penny. Being close is good enough, and spirit will provide. Another example is that the right brain imagines a picture, and the left-brain is assigned to draw it. Also, an infant's left brain notices that his mother did not pick him up, and the right brain assigns a meaning: "Perhaps she doesn't love me."

Everyone has a dominant side, and the way are raised may determine which side is dominant. For example, if we were raised to be analytical and to repress our feelings, we probably are left-brained. If we were raised to play the piano and encouraged to create new music, we likely are right-brained.

Sometimes the left and right brains get out of balance. The left-brain is action-oriented; the right brain is creative and imaginative. When we perform actions without meaning, they seem hollow. When we create things in our minds and do not act on them, we tend to spin in one place and remain stationary. At extremes, the right brain without the left-brain is powerless; the left-brain without the right brain is brutal.

How do the hemispheres get out of balance? When trauma occurs in any area, it inhibits development in that area, and the brain tries to compensate for the imbalance. For example, when a newborn infant has a breathing problem and cannot get enough oxygen, it may affect functioning on the instinctive level. If a baby feels hunger and cries out for food, but is not fed because "it is not time to feed according to the schedule," the child knows only hunger and the pain associated with it. Not being fed or going without air is traumatic to the system. The baby does not know it is "not time" for feeding. This system does not know time or rationality; it knows hunger. When the organism cannot breathe or eat, it recognizes the threat of potential destruction and produces the "fight or flight" hormones of fear.

As we grow and develop, we form emotional attachments to our parents, grandparents, siblings, aunts, uncles, etc. If these emotional needs are not met, trauma occurs. When the warmth and closeness that is needed is withheld, it creates pain and the fear of abandonment.

As we continue to develop, our needs change. The attachments to our loved ones begin to take on a different meaning. When we try our best to please them and feel it is not appreciated, trauma begins. When we are not recognized for our efforts and are expected to meet unreachable goals by over-demanding parents, it creates pain and fear—the fear of not being good enough.

Here is the dilemma: When trauma occurs in the organism, the brain produces chemicals that prevent the communication of the source of the pain from one level to the next. This defense mechanism, which is activated to enable the body to continue functioning, is called repression. An illusionary separation occurs. The brain and body, however, continue to react to the trauma unconsciously with the fight or flight response, which produces high blood pressure, a queasy stomach, tenseness, and stress.

The conscious mind does not know the real causes of the symptoms. We think they are from the present, but they are not. The feelings elicited from current events often are from the past. We react in the present to past events that drive our behavior, and invent reasons to justify the way we feel.

These reasons may be logical, but often are irrational because they are based on symbols of the real causes of the pain. For example, someone may reject us in a relationship. The rejection hurts, so we withdraw and think, "Why does this always happen? Why do people always reject me?" We search inside to find our faults and then dwell on them, thinking and feeling that we are not good enough, that we are flawed at the core. The event was: A particular person did not want to be with me. The meaning derived was: People always abandon me; therefore, I am not good enough. The meaning may be logical, but it is not rational. The real cause may be that our parents rejected us over and over, and we projected that rejection onto the current event.

Even if we understand why our parents rejected us, no amount of understanding, insights or thinking can alter the feeling, because the feeling was not generated from our thinking brain.

> *Laura has been divorced four times, and deep inside she feels the hurt and the shame she learned as a child, and believes she is a failure because she cannot maintain a relationship. Laura told us she knows everything works out for the best and that her current relationship is the best she has ever had. She admitted there is no reason to feel hurt because she is happy now, and if she had not left her former husbands, she would not be where she is now. However, no matter how much she knows these facts in her conscious mind, she still feels the hurt in her abdomen. Her thoughts are logical, but her feelings are irrational.*

Although it is true to an extent that our thinking affects who we are, this is not the case with deep-rooted, unresolved hurt. Many people believe that the hurt they feel inside is due to wrong thinking. They try to alter the way they think in order to change the way they feel, but what they do not know is the real reason they feel the way that they do. They continue to make up stories and lies about their feelings to further repress them. Unfortunately, the hurt returns—it always does until the real cause is discovered and dealt with. This is the energy of truth. Truth energy is the uninhibited flow of energy that invariably arises, wanting to be recognized and reconciled. When people think the hurt returns because of wrong thinking, they try again and again to alter their thinking patterns. They are caught in a double bind and punish themselves, continuing to believe that they are thinking incorrectly. We see this occur mostly among intellectually based men, who try to use their intellect to defend against their pain. The intellect is disconnected from the source of the pain, so how can they find the source without allowing the feelings to surface and experiencing them for what they really are?

Mickey is brilliant. For the last several years, Mickey has been searching for his true identity. Every time he gets close, the hurt inside rises to the surface and he tries to think his way out of it. He never realizes why he continues to feel the hurt because, being erudite, he has read all the right books, says all the right words, and knows all the right people. The self-help books he reads recommend affirmation after affirmation. He does them all, but to no avail. Two years ago we approached Mickey and showed him an alternative, an opportunity to discover the real causes of his hurt. Using his

*superior intellect, he surmised that the process
wasn't necessary because it was his aberrant
thinking that caused the hurt to continue. Two
years later, Mickey is still searching outside
himself. He continues to repress the feelings that
rise to the surface, although he has read a
hundred more books and tried a hundred more
methods and affirmations. He is trapped in his
own intellectual loop, with no hope until he
starts to think differently—until he goes within
and allows what he has been repressing to rise
to the surface so he can see it for what it really
is. Until then, he will lie to himself again and
again.*

External Balancing

We achieve internal balance first. Whatever we
need for augmentation from the outside, we
unconsciously will seek externally. We accomplish
external balancing through our relationships. When
our internal balance changes, our relationships
change. Not just our relationship with our spouse or
partner, but all relationships, including those with
friends, family members, employers, employees, and
the people we meet in checkout lines and elevators.

There is a difference between spiritual and
psychological balancing. Psychology is meaningless if
there is no depth through spirituality to free us to
experience deeper truths. Spirituality is groundless
without the ability of psychology to assist us with
living in this dimension. It can manifest in

grandiosity and delusion, as Howard and Mary's story demonstrates.

> *Howard is grounded. He is practical and organized, but lacks spirituality. Mary is up in the clouds. She is very spiritually motivated, but lacks practicality. By aligning themselves in a relationship, they meet each another's needs and maintain balance. After years of being together, Howard developed spirituality and Mary developed the ability to live in the third dimension. At this point they both needed other things, so the relationship broke up and each of them has aligned with others who meet their current needs.*

Relationships not only to assist us in achieving balance, they mirror who we are, reflecting our fears, love, and personalities. If we fear abandonment, we project abandonment energy with our feelings and thoughts. Since energy attracts like energy, we align ourselves with people who abandon us—or the opposite, those who are co-dependent and smothering. They will never leave us, but on the other hand, they cannot hold up their part in the relationship because they are constantly clinging to us. This happens until we break the energy patterns of abandonment and seek something else, another lesson. If we fear that we are not good enough, we may compromise or "settle" by aligning ourselves with people who do not meet our needs. Conversely, we may align with people who are so demanding that we can never meet their expectations, and thus relive the energy patterns of not being good enough. These patterns repeat themselves until we see the truth and overcome the primal fear of not being good enough.

Some of us spend our childhoods seeking recognition or attention from our parents. When the attention is not given, we alter our behavior patterns to seek it even more. Sometimes this "acting out" turns into an obsession that causes aberrant behavior. For example, Dianne's parents did not acknowledge her unless she was "bad", so she created havoc with her siblings to get attention, even though the attention was a spanking. As an adult, she has a tendency to get involved with men who beat her. To Dianne, this was a familiar feeling and she felt comfortable because she was getting attention, until she realized the source for the obsession. She has since changed the patterns in her life and married a caring, loving man.

What are the traits we seek in our mates or others with whom we associate? We seem to search for those with whom we feel comfortable. Comfortable is a relative thing; all of us want to be comfortable. What is comfortable is familiar, and a feeling that seems familiar may delude us into thinking that it is comfortable: "The devil we know is better than the devil we do not know."

For example, a woman we met always associated with men who abused her. The men in her life hated women and she loved them. We were able to help her to bring these feelings to the surface. One night after thrashing around on the floor uncontrollably, feeling the pain she had stored for decades, she had a great insight. The men she surrounded herself with were like her father—a father who abused her and, despite her efforts, could not love her for who she was. Unconsciously, she set herself up for the familiar feelings of abuse and rejection. Her relationships were doomed to failure, as was the relationship she had with her father. Now her relationships are with men who are more caring and gentle. She chooses the relationships consciously now, not through the compulsive behavior of the unconscious past. The "acting out" by choosing abusive men like her father always pointed to the truth that her father did not love her for who she was. The feelings associated with her recent abusive relationships were linked to the feelings associated with her perceived loss of fatherly love. This was her truth.

The comfort level we maintain in these relationships is one of numbness. The more we repress our true feelings, the more we are subject to our compulsive, irrational behaviors. Some people think that feelings are irrational, but feelings are part of our rationality. They have logic in themselves. Feelings are different from emotions. Real feeling is love-based and is a response to the present experience. Emotions are fear-based and are reactions to the present filtered through past experiences. Emotions are generated by anxiety. Anxiety is anachronistic fear based on past experiences. It is a repression of true feeling—when we say we are feeling anxiety, we actually are not feeling at all. Anxiety triggers emotions, and emotional behavior may be confused with real feeling. When we repress the pain that brings up our feelings, it seems as if we are "normal." The more we repress, the more "normal" we are. What hypocrisy! In our society, it seems as if those who control the way they act and feel are those who are considered normal. Normal as compared to *what*?

As children, we learn to control our expressions. How many of us have heard, "Don't show them how you feel." Why not? Because people will take advantage of us? Because if they think we are hurt, they will hurt us more? So we hide ourselves, fall asleep, and walk around like zombies. We build walls so high that when we look up, we can barely see sunlight. Even worse, our parents may tell us that the way we are feeling is wrong: "You shouldn't feel like that!" they say.

Many religions try to make us feel guilty for our thoughts and feelings. We are told to confess our sins to the Creator through a priest or minister, when deep down inside we don't think our thoughts or feelings are sins. Since each of us views reality from a different perspective, we do not do things that we consider bad or sinful. We use defense mechanisms such as rationalization and compartmentalization to justify our actions. For example, we may steal from an employer, not thinking it is wrong because we have rationalized that the employer is underpaying us or that he deserved it because he makes more money than we do.

We are constantly barraged with judgment about the ways we think and feel. We start to believe there is something wrong with us for the way we think and feel, so we become guilty and try to repress our thoughts and feelings even further. It's a vicious circle that leads to unhappiness and dissatisfaction with ourselves. Working with the Enneagram can provide us with tools to recognize our strengths and better understand our challenges.

The Enneagram and Balance

There are three triads in the Enneagram that represent areas of potential imbalance. The Nine, Three, and Six anchor these areas. The Nine is the center of the Instinctual (Body) triad that includes the One and the Eight. The Three is the center of the Feeling (Heart) triad that includes the Two and the Four. The Six is the center of the Thinking (Mind) Triad that includes the Five and the Seven. If someone is in the Feeling triad, this does not mean he is more emotional than someone in the Thinking or Instinctual triads. Each of the triads represent an area that the ego identifies with, which may be the area that is most distorted in functioning.

As noted above, all three areas seek balance within themselves and with others. Each area interacts with and affects the other areas. If one area is out of balance, the other areas compensate for the imbalance. All there is, is Essence: a flow of energy. When the energy flow gets distorted or blocked, then the balance is distorted and blocked.

The Instinctual (Body-Based) Triad

The Eight, Nine, and One are concerned with maintaining boundaries with the environment based on physical tension. They accomplish this through aggression and repression, thus creating rage. The Eight acts out the rage, the Nine denies it, and the One represses it.

Growth in the Instinctual triad promotes grounded stability and functioning in the third dimension. Without growth in this triad, boundaries develop, creating a false sense of self. Usually there is an energy restriction centered somewhere in the body. The One, Eight, and Nine use their wills to affect the outside world. They build walls or boundaries that can be directed outwardly, inwardly, or both.

Type One: Ones maintain their energy boundaries internally. They repress their impulses in an effort to maintain the image of being "good little boys and girls." If the impulses were to surface, they would seriously affect the "good" status, and thus create internal criticism.

Type Eight: Eights, in contrast to Ones, direct energy outward, against the environment. The best defense is a good offense. Their energy boundaries are expansive as a defense to keep people away from them because when people get close, the Eight gets hurt. They are the "bad boys and girls" of the Enneagram.

Type Nine: Nines strives for peace and harmony both internally and externally, thus their instinctual energies go both ways. They are stuck between the "bad boys and girls" of the Eight and the "good boys and girls" of the One. Like the Eight, they try to control the external environment by creating energy boundaries to keep people away. Like the One, they create internal boundaries to maintain inner peace and harmony. The amount of energy expended creating dual boundaries often fatigues the Nine.

The Feeling (Heart-Based) Triad

The Two, Three, and Four are concerned with self-image and what others think of them. They identify with these images so much that they think the images they project are who they really are. The primary issue with this triad is shame. Thinking there is something wrong with them (and the perceived loss of Essence) creates shame. Twos avoid shame by being good, Threes avoid shame by being perfect and efficient in accomplishments, and Fours avoid shame by seeing themselves as victims and creating dramatic displays.

Growth in the Feeling triad manifests as the emergence of the real self. We know who we are, and it has nothing to do with what people think of us. Essence energy flows through us when the heart is open. It is like a channeling of the Creator. Without growth, we create a false sense of self through projected images. In the Feeling triad, when the false self is not recognized, hostility may result.

Type Two: Twos strive to be needed by others. They confuse (and identify) needing with love. They focus their energies against the environment and towards people in an effort to meet others' needs. As a result, they lose connection with their own feelings and needs. They are rescuers.

Type Four: Fours maintain their false images by going inward, creating fantasies and sad stories. They develop a victim mentality, and want to be rescued by the "knight in shining armor" who will see them as special and unique. This attitude may get them attention in the form of pity. They will create moods and feelings rather than to allow what is within to arise.

Type Three: Threes, like Twos, project their energy outward, seeking value through accomplishments. They are quick to sense what others want, and like chameleons, will change to present the successful image. Like Fours, they will internalize trying to see themselves, and thus may believe they are their images. Threes are stuck between the hysterical Twos and the depressive, withdrawn Fours.

The Thinking (Head-Based) Triad

The Fives, Sixes, and Sevens are concerned with lack of support and guidance, creating anxiety. Thinking that support is not available in the environment, Fives withdraw into cerebral constructs. Sixes look for strong authoritative people (like lost fathers) who will support them. Sevens are gluttonous and will strive after superficial experiences, seeking happiness.

Growth in this triad creates a quiet mind—a mind allowed to know support and guidance from the universe, seeing object reality as it is. Without growth, anxiety and insecurity rise to the surface, creating a mind that does not stop to rest and an incessant chattering. For those in this triad, centering in the body is very important for growth.

Type Five: Fives are stingy with their energy, and tend to retreat from the world into their cerebral constructs where they feel safe. They will stay within until they think they possess enough knowledge to function in the external world.

Type Seven: Sevens project their energy outward. They seek experiences in the outside world that will bring them happiness. Without the internal depth, they find the external world shallow and devoid of meaning, and always are striving for more excitement.

Type Six: Sixes are stuck between the vivacious Sevens and the stingy, withdrawn Fives. Sixes, like Sevens, project outward when anxiety is internal, looking for satisfaction externally. Then they get scared, and like Fives, withdraw into inner world constructs. The movement back and forth creates an enormous energy drain.

Hornevian Groups:

The late psychiatrist Karen Horney identified three ways people react socially with others, and with the environment, to meet their needs. The three ways are assertiveness, compliance, and withdrawal. Each of the nine Enneatypes falls into one of these groups: the Assertives, the Compliants, and the Withdrawns. The Assertives may be called people of fire, because fire is aggressive and can get out of control, just like the Assertives. Fire reacts against the environment by destroying it. The Compliants may be called people of water. Water is complaint and molds itself to the container that holds it. Though water behind a dam may seem weak, in the long run, it will overtake the dam and spill out. The Withdrawns could be called people of ice, for ice is cold and withdrawn. Fire melts ice, which turns to water and becomes compliant.

Each group reacts differently to the environment as a defense mechanism in order for the false self or ego to meet its needs. In a balanced situation, the three groups react to the environment depending on the external stimuli and the internal interpretation to those stimuli. If we experience object reality without ego filters, we are like clear mirrors: we react to the environment in each moment, without judgment or comparison. Lacking that balance, the ego reacts in accordance with the defense mechanism of the Enneatype.

The Assertives:

Hornevian Groups – Assertives

Assertives	Heart Point	Stress Point
Eight	Two – Compliant	Five - Withdrawn
Three	Six – Compliant	Nine - Withdrawn
One	Seven – Compliant	Four - Withdrawn

The Assertive group includes Enneatypes One, Three, and Eight. Assertives move against people and the environment; they are expansive; inflate the ego, and direct energy outward. Accustomed to having their own way, they make things happen rather than allow things to happen and flow. They are the "movers and the shakers"—the doers. In groups they need to be the center of attention and want to dominate the group. Eights openly try to control groups through strength and intimidation; they are loud and have expansive, intrusive energy. Ones initially do not move outward, but eventually they expand and tend to moralize and preach their own versions of perfectionism.[5] Threes expand outward to be the center of attention, but they do so while cognizant of how other people feel about them.

Every Enneatype is connected to the others through Stress Points and Heart Points (sometimes called Paths of Disintegration and Paths of Integration), which are discussed in detail later in the book.) In the Assertives group, each of the types move to a Compliant Heart Point when at ease or relaxed: One moves to Seven, Three moves to Six, and Eight moves to Two. With internal peace and growth, the Assertives move to more complaint behavior characteristics; this includes giving in to others and being of service to people. At the Stress Point, Assertives move to Withdrawn types when experiencing stress that cannot be handled within that Enneatype's behavior. One moves to Four, Three moves to Nine, and Eight moves to Five. With undue stress, Assertives withdraw from the environment, lick their wounds, and try to regroup. They may

---

[5] Traditionally, Enneatype Seven, rather than Enneatype One, was associated with this grouping. On the surface, the Seven appears assertive in trying to experience everything, but the deeper desires of Enneatype Sevens put them in the Complaint group. Sevens initially, expand and love to be the center of attention in groups, but under the surface, they want to do their own thing with a compliant, "live and let live" attitude.

think that love is not attainable outside and withdraw inside.

Traditionally, the Heart Point is associated with growth and integration of the soul, while and the Stress Point is connected with disintegration. However, those going to the Heart Point may exhibit the dysfunctional behavior of the Heart Point Enneatype, and those moving to the Stress Point may exhibit the positive behavior of the Stress Point Enneatype. It depends on the level of evolution and growth of the individual in the now timeframe.

The Compliants:

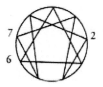

Hornevian Groups – Compliants

Compliants	Heart Point	Stress Point
Two	Four - Withdrawn	Eight - Assertive
Six	Nine - Withdrawn	Three - Assertive
Seven	Five - Withdrawn	One - Assertive

The Compliant group includes Enneatypes Two, Six, and Seven. These types move toward people and want to be of service to others. Compliants are always looking for the right thing to do, and give in to others to attain love (although giving in to others may be at their own expense). They have a tendency to project a sense of superiority over other people. For example, Twos need to be needed, and in that strategy they project, "I am better than you are, and you need my help." On the surface, Sevens are expansive, happy-go-lucky types, but underneath and unconsciously, they project a snobbish, "better than you" attitude—an attitude of entitlement. Sixes identify with groups or belief systems for security purposes and use the group or "ism" to project an attitude of superiority: "I belong to the Association."

At the Heart Points, Compliants move to Withdrawn types. Two moves to Four, Six moves to Nine, and Seven moves to Five. This means that with inner peace and growth, Complaints move to Withdrawn behavior characteristics that allow them to withdraw and take care of their own needs. At the Stress Point, Compliants move to the Assertive behavior characteristics: Two moves to Eight, Six moves to Three, and Seven moves to One. When experiencing undue stress, they lash out at others with the intent of pulling people back in. But ironically, with this type of behavior they tend to push people farther away.

The Withdrawns:

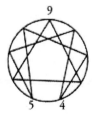

Hornevian Groups – Withdrawns

Withdrawns	Heart Point	Stress Point
Four	One - Assertive	Two - Compliant
Five	Eight - Assertive	Seven - Compliant
Nine	Three - Assertive	Six - Compliant

    The Withdrawn group includes Enneatypes Four, Five, and Nine. They move away from people and the environment into their inner world, which seems as real to them as the outer world. In the inner world, the Withdrawns feel safer. Fours move to their romantically fantasized world of self, Fives move into their complex cerebral virtual reality where they try to make sense of life, and Nines move to their safe inner sanctum. Being Withdrawn, all of them have trouble "doing" —going into action. Withdrawns are happier when they are in their home environment, alone.

    At the Heart Point, Withdrawns move to Assertive behavior characteristics: Four moves to One, Five moves to Eight; and Nine moves to Three. With inner peace and growth, they feel comfortable enough to come out of their shells and meet the environment head-on. At the Stress Point, Withdrawns adopt Compliant behavior characteristics: Four moves to Two, Five moves to

Seven, and Nine moves to Six. When experiencing undue stress, Withdrawns tend to take the "I don't care; whatever you want is fine," stance. This allows them the time and space to keep the peace and withdraw further into their inner realities.

5 The Importance of Movement

Many of us think that healing means living life free of pain and suffering. Just the fact that we live in our bodies, and our bodies are limited in the third dimension, means we will experience pain. When we stub our toe, it hurts. When we touch a hot stove, our hand hurts. When a loved one dies, it hurts. That is the way it is, and there is nothing we can do about it except to experience it. Healing is realigning ourselves with ourselves, being who we really are, and living our lives from a base of love rather than fear. This is easy to say, and many people say it. But how many people do we know that actually do it? Knowing that we must live our lives through love is awareness, and living our lives through love is consciousness.

When we lose connection with the All-That-Is, our consciousness bifurcates and creates unconsciousness to hide the pain associated with being disconnected from its source. The unconsciousness contains the key for restoration and unity; it is where the truth is hidden. The consciousness is fooled into thinking that nothing has been lost, and it does not understand that full potential as a human being can be achieved only with reintegration. So, how do we transform awareness into consciousness? How do we return to that loving being to which we were born?

The Enneagram dynamics assist us in recognizing what happened to us. We were born as expressions of loving Essence, centered in the Enneagram – I AM. Consciousness was created so that we could experience the wonders of the universe through the illusion of individuality. The expression of self in a loving way reflects the clear, undistorted images of objective reality, so that we may experience the wonders as they truly are. Due to the rejection we experienced as children (which is often repeated throughout our lives), we fall asleep to who we really are and strive to regain love by pretending to be someone we think others will accept.

Falling asleep to who we really are, we enter the Enneagram of personality at Enneatype Nine. We are afraid of making waves; afraid to do anything for fear that we may further lose love. We feel insignificant and unappreciated, as if we were nobody special. We fear doing, thinking that we will make mistakes. When we realize that we must do something, we go into motion, albeit with fear (Enneatype Six). Thinking it would be better when we act to pretend to be someone else (so that we may avoid responsibility for our actions), we move to Enneatype Three: we put on a different face and project an image that is not our real self. Realizing deceit to others and to our true nature at Enneatype Three, we fall further asleep and move back to Enneatype Nine, where we may repeat the pattern endlessly. At any point in this process, we may fixate and gravitate to one of the main three Enneatypes (the Nine, Six, or Three).

Alternatively, we may move to one of the wings in either direction, and identify and fixate on that personality. (For more information on the wings, see Chapters 6 through 14 on the Enneagram types) For example, entering the personality at the Nine, we may experience inner rage, and then move to the type Eight personality and project expansive, shielding energy outwardly onto the environment. Recognizing that this may be a valid strategy for protection, we may choose to fixate and remain at Enneatype Eight. This process occurs unconsciously because we are asleep, and are looking for any way to be safe and find the love we think we have lost.

Fixations and Passions

Enneatypes and Their Fixations / Passions

Type	Fixation / Passion	Heart Point	Stress Point
One	Anger / Resentment	Seven	Four
Two	Pride / Flattery	Four	Eight
Three	Vanity / Deceit	Six	Nine
Four	Envy / Melancholy	One	Two
Five	Avarice / Stinginess	Eight	Seven
Six	Fear (Anxiety) / Cowardice	Nine	Three
Seven	Gluttony / Planning	Five	One
Eight	Lust/ Vengeance	Two	Five
Nine	Sloth (Indolence}/ Sloth	Three	Six

Fixations of the Enneatype occur as the ego develops and takes control over the personality. When we are born, we have everything we need. We are filled with love, warmth, trust, and faith. At the deepest levels, we have spiritual perspectives to existence. We are connected with the All-That-Is, and this connection provides depth to our essential natures. As we perceive loss of connection to Essence through painful life experiences, we develop dependence on the ego structure in order to survive. Ego structures contain fixed ideas or delusions of how we are flawed (shame), how we should act, and what we should believe. These ideas are filtered through the illusory smoke and fog of ego structures that distort reality. As ego develops further and our dependence on it is solidified, we fixate more and more at the points of the Enneagram and away from the center of it.

Ego fixations create lies and distortions of reality, and these fixations become paramount to our essential selves. As we view reality, we see contradictions between the way we think the world should be and how it actually is. Filtered through the ego, the fixations connect to emotional charges that are obsessive, compulsive, and unconscious. They are ways of emoting while truth is hidden, and are known as passions. Passions develop as automatic responses to denial of the way things are. For example, resentment, the passion of the One Enneatype, is connected to suppression and repression of anger, the fixation of the One. Ones, trying to be "good boys and girls," know that expression of anger does not coincide with their view of perfection, so they suppress or repress the anger. Repressed anger creates internal rage, and this rage can be expressed in different ways. The One expresses it internally, and rage develops into resentment.

Below is a brief summary of each Enneatype, its fixations, and its passions.

One: Anger / Resentment - They fear going out of control. When they were children, they had to repress their anger at not being allowed to be themselves. Repressed anger causes rage and is expressed by Ones as resentment. Ones resent others behaving in "imperfect" ways while they suffer, trying to be good. This is a form of martyrdom. Anger is seen as weakness and not perfection, so it is suppressed or repressed by the One. Resentment arises from not expressing anger when they realize there is a difference between the way life is and how it can be. Ones do not know they are angry, and exhibit this emotion in the stiffness of the body. Anger is the One's false core belief of not accepting reality as it is—it is a resistance to reality.

Two: Pride / Flattery - They fear the humiliation of not being needed by others. As children, they learned to flatter others to get attention and pseudo-love, resulting in a distorted sense of self. They need to be the source of love to everyone else. Flattery is a strategy they use to get their way by manipulating others. If they do not get their way (if people reject their help), they feel a sense of hurt. This creates pride: "How can they not need me? See what I do for them? They are ungrateful!" Pride is the Two's false core belief thinking that others do not need their help or that Twos do not need others to help them. Interdependent connection to source is lost.

Three: Vanity / Deceit - They fear humiliation and not being good enough if they fail to achieve what they set out to achieve. They need to be the best and look good in doing so. As children, they were valued for their achievements and found that they had to "do" to get recognition and love. Threes created an efficiency of style so they could achieve more. This strategy resulted in self-deceit: Threes think they are separate doers (demigods) from the natural unfolding of the universe. They lost the trust in universal unfolding, resulting in vanity—thinking they need to initiate doing and do not trust in natural unfolding. They confuse their identities with their projected images, believing that what they do is who they are. In doing so, they present to the world (and to themselves) a deceitful, non-genuine self that they think is real. Vanity is the Three's false core belief thinking that "I must do it, or it will not get done." It is the loss of connection to natural doing.

Four: Envy / Melancholy - They fear abandonment. As children, they lost the deep sense of connection to universal source (Essence) and felt abandoned, which led to a state of melancholy. They live with the belief that this separation happened only to them and not everyone else, and focus on what is missing in life. They pine for what others have that they feel they lack, even to the point of destroying good in the world: if they cannot have something, no one else will either. This is envy, the Four's false core belief thinking that if they cannot have connection with Essence, then no one should have it.

Five: Avarice / Stinginess - They fear being incompetent. As children, they learned to seek love through their ability to accumulate knowledge. When they were threatened, they developed protective strategies by withdrawing into their inner world and trying to figure out life with their minds. This strategy produces stinginess with energy, time, and knowledge. They feel they do not have enough energy, time, and knowledge, so they develop the defense mechanism of compartmentalization, keeping facets of their lives separated. Compartmentalization allows them to control and manipulate their environment. Avarice is the Five's false core belief thinking that if they do not accumulate knowledge (or material items), they will not have enough time to figure out life, and thus will be incompetent.

Six: Fear (Anxiety) / Cowardice - They fear having no support and guidance in the environment and are afraid that people will turn against them, ruining their safety and security. As children, they lost their sense of security by having to remain alert to dangers in the environment. They developed cowardice by not allowing themselves to fully engage in life with the knowledge that they will be protected and secure. They lost their faith in the security of

Essence (that everything will work out) and developed doubt that they will be safe by letting go and being themselves. Fear (anxiety) is Sixes' false core belief thinking that they will not be protected in the environment if they surrender to it.

Seven: Gluttony / Planning - They fear being deprived of happiness and trapped in internal pain. As children, they learned to take care of themselves and focus on distractions like games, toys, and playmates. They learned to keep moving and to experience everything they can at high superficial energy levels, avoiding internal meaning and depth. Sevens spend much of their time planning future events that continues the strategy of escaping from inner reality. They learned to fill themselves up with things and experiences. Gluttony is the Seven's false core belief thinking that quantity rather than quality of experience is more important. It is tasting, but never fully digesting, life experiences.

Eight: Lust / Vengeance - They fear being harmed or controlled by other people. As children, they learned that the strong dominated the weak, and that being controlled by others meant they would be seen as weak. To defend themselves against pain, they learned vengeance, believing in "an eye for an eye," and that it would be better to "get them before they get me" (the best defense is a strong offense). They realized that power and energy projected outwardly allowed them a lustful pursuit to meet their needs and keep their expansive, broad boundaries. To feel alive, Eights do everything with intensity or lustfulness. Lust is the Eight's false core belief thinking that they are so strong that they can live their lives at extremes without any consequences.

Nine: Sloth (Indolence) / Sloth - They fear losing peace and harmony both internally and externally. This fear is so great that they are willing to cut themselves off from emotions and feelings in order to maintain an emotional straight line. They do not want to engage internally in what they are doing, and tend to look as if they are going through the motions. They have difficulty identifying priorities. Sloth is the Nine's false core belief that thinking they are so insignificant that there is nothing they can do, so they fall asleep to their Essential selves.

Energy Movement

Once locked in at a personality type, we follow the energy flow back and forth from that Enneatype to the Heart and Stress Points. When type Eight is relaxed and comfortable, for example, he moves to the Heart Point of Enneatype Two, and gives more to others. He does not become a Two, but he does show positive traits of the Two. When experiencing undue stress, the Eight moves to the safety of type Five (Stress Point) and withdraws into his inner world to lick his wounds and regroup. Regardless of whether the Eight moves to the Heart or Stress Points, he still anchors at type Eight and will always return there. The same is true for all the other personality types.

In Enneagram theory, the more the types move to their Heart Point (Path of Integration), the more evolved or healthy they are. Conversely, the more the types move to their Stress Point, the more unevolved or unhealthy they are. In the mid-range of evolvement or healthy type, the personality seems to anchor at its home Enneatype. It depends upon how much the ego is driving the personality: the more ego, the less evolved or unhealthy the person; the less ego, the more evolved or healthy. At the healthiest level, with ego minimized, the personality lives the positive attributes of its type and Heart Point and becomes self-actualized. These people appear genuine, loving, and balanced; they are mature and are very well functioning. At its unhealthiest, with ego maximized, the personality lives the negative attributes of its type and Stress Point and becomes highly dysfunctional, with symptoms of personality instability. Such people have strong defenses and difficulty coping in the world. Their fear intensifies, and a full abandonment of self-results. We may choose to evolve or dissolve, so to speak.

Evolvement, or moving toward self-actualization, does not mean finding out who we are and what we need to do to exhibit traits of the Heart Point types. This would just be the ego playing games with us, making us think we are growing, when in fact we are acting out. The ego's intent would be dominant, and the acting out would be narcissistic and self-promoting. For example, if the type Three recognizes himself as a type Three, he knows that in moving to the Heart Point of type Six he should exhibit character traits he may think of as growth. He may present these traits (teamwork, loyalty, persistence, etc.) in order to further advance his career and make other people think he is growing. In this example, the Three is not really moving to a Heart Point, but manifests positive behaviors driven by his ego's desire to appear healthy and present a good image. He has not progressed in development; he moved to the Six with narcissistic intent. This move is called moving to the Security Point. If the type Three, through inner reflection and love, moves to the Heart Point of type Six and genuinely lives these traits through his own personality, then he is not acting out; he is truly growing. The difference is the intent—intent driven by ego is always a fear reaction. In this example, the type Three thinks that to promote himself, he must exhibit traits of what others may consider personal growth. It does not mean he has grown; it means he is acting the part of growth and fears rejection due to not growing. This is deceitful not only to oneself but to other people, and deceit is the passion of the Enneatype Three.

Real potential for growth occurs when the Enneatype moves to the Stress Point. Movement to the Stress Point occurs when we cannot cope by using the characteristic defense for our Enneatype because the intensity of the stress is too overwhelming. When we get to this level, it is the same as moving to the Security Point and acting out. This is unconscious and compulsive. The Enneagram is a flow of energy, and energy needs to flow freely without suppression or repression. We may choose to cling to the energy of events in our lives and trap the energy of those events, which prevents the free flow. Imagine nine people sitting around a huge globe, looking forward. All anyone can see is the countries in front of them. This is all they know; it is their worldview. What they are missing is the rest of the global perspective. We may say that what they see is like what each Enneatype sees: only one perspective of the whole. They all are looking at the same thing but are seeing it in different ways. With this perspective, their experiences are filtered by what they know.

Everything that happens is interpreted internally based on our past experiences, and is projected through the filters of the present moment. When we experience stress, it is due to a truth that we suppressed or repressed that is rising to the surface. It may present itself as stress, anxiety, and uneasiness, but it is truth wanting to be recognized and resolved. Stress is triggered by external events to which we have assigned meaning based on past events or future expectations. We have judged or compared the event to something in another period of time. By doing this, we miss the perfection in the current moment. We miss the wonder of trust that all is for the best and highest good, even though we may not see it at the time. We lose our faith in the highest good of the universe and the trust that by letting go, we will be cared for. By comparing an event to what happened in the past, we judge the current event with the suppressed or repressed emotions of a past event. These emotions frequently are associated with traumatic events because we choose to cling to the energy of those events (which masks itself as fear) rather than live through it and allow it to pass. If love is all there is, what are we afraid of from the past?

Were we not loved? Were we not allowed to be ourselves? Are we flawed?

In objective reality, there is no such thing as fear. The fear we experience is the fear we created through false core beliefs of not being good enough to be ourselves. If we created them, we can un-create them.

At the Stress Point, we need to examine the root cause of the stress, which can be accessed through the emotions driving the stress and the underlying feelings. We need to remember that we are rarely upset about what we think we are upset about; it usually is deeper. It is very difficult to transform this energy at the Stress Point, but at these times, we are closest to the truth. It takes inner work to know when we are there, and courage to allow the truth to be seen and reconciled for what it really is. We realize that the only thing to fear is the fear that our ego created. Truth was and will always be there. Love was and will always be there. The truth will set us free— free to manifest who we truly are, free to be ourselves, free to love and be loved, free to mirror the wonderful creation of the universe and to experience its sweetness, integrity, warmth, and love.

When reconciling truth at the Stress Point, we find that love fills all the holes, and we have let go of something we were clinging to. This process automatically propels us back to our Enneatype and moves us further into the Heart Point, Path of Integration. It is so automatic that we do not have to try and move to the Heart Point; it just happens. The more we do this, the more we find automatic, innate flows of energy all around the Enneagram. We find that we are not limited to our main Enneatype, its wings, and the Heart and Stress Points. When we are not restricted by self-induced repression, we find positive energy flows as we reacquire the energy and love of the universe. We are free to flow.

In reconciliation of the truth contained at the Stress Point, we find that the negative attributes associated with the Stress Point is converted and transformed to positive attributes. For example, Eights who move to the Stress Point of the Five withdraw. Negatively, Eights use this time to lick their wounds and regroup; usually thinking of strategies for vengeance against those they feel drove them to the point of stress. They look externally for others to blame. Realizing the truth of the stress and reconciling it, they may exhibit positive traits of the Five: inner reflection and conservation of energy.

Stress Points

One: When experiencing undue stress, Ones move to Four. Overburdened by their incessant striving for relative perfection and feeling that no one else appreciates them, they start to fantasize and daydream of what they lack that others possess. "Why do others get away with things and I do not? How come I am the only one who is responsible? Why do I pay the price and others do not?" At the Four, Ones often lose their self-control and express strong emotions as anger and resentments arise. In the move to Four, Ones may further deteriorate and use their anger to be "bad little boys or girls." They may become self-indulgent, thinking that they have earned it, or blame others for their fury: "You made me get angry!"

When the anger arises internally, Ones can recognize the source of the anger: not being allowed to be who they truly are, feeling they are not good enough, being expected to fit other people's ideas of "good," and listening to the omnipresent critical voice in their head that actually sounds like someone else. As truth is reconciled, Ones may experience positive traits of the Four: creativity and deep feeling. In letting go, Ones are propelled back to the One position, plus automatically move to the Heart Point, Path of Integration of the Seven. At the Seven, Ones have fun, experience life without being tense, see that there are other possibilities associated with perfection, and realize that perfection is not limited to what they think it is.

Two: When experiencing undue stress, Twos move to Eight. Sensing that people do not appreciate the things they do for them, do not need their help, and may abandon them, Twos reveal toughness at Eight. They may challenge those they blame for the stress by being confrontational like the Eight. They can be aggressive and strong, and may threaten others with abandonment or major lawsuits. If they continue to deteriorate at the Eight, Twos will push away their loved ones and experience abandonment themselves. They will get what they fear most: that people do not need them.

When their pride is hurt, Twos can notice the feeling internally and allow the source of the hurt to surface, where they can see it and reconcile the energy associated with it. They may recognize hurt pride from the feeling of not being allowed to be themselves and have their own needs met, catering to others for the recognition and love they already possess, and not believing they are good enough to meet their own needs internally. As the truth is revealed and reconciled, Twos may experience positive traits of the Eight: taking care of themselves and feeling independent. In letting go of pride, Twos are propelled back to the Two point, plus automatically move to the Heart Point, Path of Integration at the Four. They experience authentic feelings of creativity and selfishness. (Selfishness is not necessarily negative, as many people believe. At this level, it can be very positive to take care of ourselves.)

Three: When experiencing undue stress, Threes move to Nine. Questioning their value in the world, they may think there is no true happiness in achievements. They may feel the elation of an accomplishment, but the joy is short-lived, and they need more and more as they relentlessly pursue love through achievements and recognition. They become disillusioned, and if they continue to deteriorate, will "zone out" and become apathetic, accomplishing nothing and living out their worst fear of being worthless.

At this low point, Threes who observe their inner realities will look for the cause of the disillusionment. They may find it in the deceitful facade they present to the world and to themselves. They may realize the truth in the pain of feeling they are not allowed to be themselves and always must accomplish things—the pain of feeling not good enough, which compels them to relentlessly pursue something they can never accomplish. As truth is revealed and reconciled, Threes may experience positive traits of the Nine: they connect with themselves and their feelings. Realizing they do not have to accomplish anything to be worthwhile, they let go of vanity and deceit and are propelled back to the Three point, plus automatically move to the Heart Point, Path of Integration at the Six. They experience being a team player and having loyalty to coworkers, friends, and family. They commit to goals and to people, a commitment that is genuine rather than self-promoting. They present themselves as themselves, not as what they think other people want to see.

Four: When experiencing undue stress, Fours move to Two. Realizing that their withdrawal from the world is causing undue stress, especially in the way they handle relationships in a push-pull style, they move to the Stress Point of Two. They move out of their shells and romanticized fantasies to reality, striving to correct their loneliness by contrived friendliness and flattery. In deterioration, they may try too hard, even dramatizing melodramatically to find out if others love them. In this manner, they will drive away their significant others and thus experience what they fear most: abandonment.

Fours who observe their behavior and allow the truth in the stress to arise may recognize its source and reconcile the energy associated with it.

They may recognize that other people do not have more than they do; Essence in the universe is omnipresent and never abandoned them. They are unique and special within themselves and do not need to be rescued. As truth is revealed and reconciled, Fours may experience positive traits of the Two: openness and deep caring for others, appreciation for what they have, and humility. In letting go of envy, Fours are propelled back to the Four point, plus automatically move to the Heart Point, Path of Integration at the One. Here they recognize the value in who they are, become productive, and stop dramatizing and emoting.

Five: When experiencing undue stress, Fives move to Seven. Realizing that withdrawing into their inner sanctum is not working, their minds speed up and they move to the Seven. At the Stress Point of Seven, they distract themselves with activity, albeit meaningless and scattered. They may become irritated, sarcastic, and insecure in their relationships. If the stress persists, they may increase their activities, searching for stimulation. At this point, they may find the meaningless chores and activities and the sarcasm expressed to loved ones will get them what they fear most: incompetence.

Fives are observers, and seeing themselves react at the Stress Point and allow truth to arise to be reconciled may help them recognize several facts. They may find that being greedy with energy and time has shut them down to meaningful relationships, that they never lost the time and space they deserved, and that they already possess the knowledge they need to function and survive. As the truth is revealed and reconciled, Fives may experience positive traits of the Seven: spontaneity, outward energy, and fulfilling experiences—traits that are difficult for the Five to express. In letting go of avarice, Fives are propelled back to the Five point, plus automatically move to the Heart Point, Path of Integration at the Eight. Here they experience instinctual body energy, and create an energy movement that feels strong. They are present with their feelings and reactions.

Six: When experiencing undue stress, Sixes move to Three. When Sixes' security comes crashing down, they panic and move to the Stress Point of Three. They become driven, work hard, and are concerned about the image they project. As they develop an intensified false image (deceit), they push harder for security, even to the point of lying about their accomplishments. At this stage, they may sabotage the structures around them with increased phobias, and thus realize their greatest fear: insecurity.

If Sixes can stop and observe fear arising, they can allow the source of the fear to surface and be reconciled. They may find that they were not allowed to be themselves, and that the environment of the universe is safe. There is nothing to doubt or question, just relaxation of the chattering mind. As truth is revealed and reconciled, Sixes may experience positive traits of the Three: they feel a genuineness of self and are productive and self-accepting. In letting go of fear, Sixes are propelled back to the Six point, plus automatically move to the Heart Point, Path of Integration at the Nine. Here they experience the positive traits of the Nine: instinctual body energy that helps them to be grounded and feel innate strength and balance. They become more present and relax in the environment.

Seven: When experiencing undue stress, Sevens move to One. Feeling emptiness in their chaotic and scattered lifestyle, increasing boredom, and unfulfilled goals, they tighten up and restrain themselves at the Stress Point of One. Bottling up their enthusiasm, Sevens at One become increasingly irritated, sarcastic, and nitpicking. They tend to preach, like the One. Deteriorating further, Sevens realize that pain still haunts them from within, so they increase their activity and panic, over-driving their minds to the point where they live their worst fear: being trapped in pain.

If Sevens can stop and observe the pain in deprivation, truth arises and they may realize that being oneself includes internal reality and feelings, that they were good enough and did not have to grow up too fast, and that things are not substitutes for happiness. Happiness is part of the journey, not a goal for those who superficially experience the most. Quality of experience is more rewarding than quantity of experience. As truth is revealed and reconciled, Sevens may experience positive traits of the One: balance and strength in the body, wisdom, and integrity of self. Letting go of the gluttony of experience, Sevens are propelled back to the Seven point, plus automatically move to the Heart Point,

Path of Integration at the Five. They experience a slowing down of activity, a quieter mind, and getting the most from experiences at deeper levels. They observe themselves and others with the realization of a cornucopia of depth and happiness.

Eight: When experiencing undue stress, Eights move to Five. Realizing that their desire for control and power (and their methods of dealing with people by bullying them) is not working, Eights move to the Stress Point of Five. They withdraw into themselves to lick their wounds and regroup, searching for ways to get back at those who challenge their strength. They brood and remain secretive. Deteriorating further, they can become irritated and caustic, attacking rivals, exacting vengeance, and pushing significant others away from them. They realize their worst fear: losing strength and control.

Eights who allow the real cause of the hurt to arise may find that the best control is no control, and that being themselves does not mean overdoing security to the point of projecting expansive energy. They understand that they react before thinking because as children in a hostile environment, they learned to attack first. As truth is revealed and reconciled, Eights may experience positive traits of the Five: they focus on their inner world and relax their minds; they become compassionate. In letting go of lust, Eights are propelled back to the Eight point, plus automatically move to the Heart Point, Path of Integration at the Two. They experience openness of feeling, deep caring and concern for others, and tenderness for themselves and others.

Nine: When experiencing undue stress, Nines move to the Stress Point of Six. They realize that staying in their inner sanctum at all costs is not productive and not working—the chaos continues no matter how much they move to straight-line emotional responses. Here they experience scattered and frantic activity. There is no time to get everything done, and everyone seems to be demanding something from them. They search for meaning in relationships or belief systems. Deteriorating, they recognize their unhappiness, and the chaos continues. Passive aggressive behavior is abandoned, and rage may surface. They blame others for the increased stress. At Six, they can be paranoid and extremely doubting. They may lose any semblance of who they are and any sense of reality that remains. Here they will experience their worst fear: annihilation.

Nines may stop and notice the feelings of anger that exploded from sloth, which contain the truth that needs to be seen and reconciled. They may recognize that their lives and opinions do count—that they are good enough and have many qualities that are constructive and meaningful. They understand that they can be seen and heard rather than lapsing into the slothfulness that developed in childhood. As the truth is revealed and reconciled, Nines may experience positive traits of the Six: they are outgoing and friendly, secure with themselves, and serene. In letting go of sloth, Nines are propelled back to the Nine Point, plus automatically move to the Heart Point, Path of Integration at the Three. Here they experience high energy, focus on tasks, and want to be loved for who they are rather than attempting to submerge their personality to blend with those around them. They find that their ideas and feelings are authentic and meaningful.

Thinking, Feeling, and Doing Centers

Within each of us is a combination of thinking, feeling, and doing, regardless of which triad of the Enneagram we fall into. As fixations are developed through the ego, thinking, feeling, and doing get out of balance, further supporting the ego fixation. For example, Eights do before they think, which in many cases is due to being raised in an environment with violence. They learned to avoid being hurt by reacting first. If they thought about reacting to a punch, for instance, it would have been too late to deflect the blow. Until they grow spiritually, Eights go through life satisfying themselves, not caring much about other people. This "not caring" is a symptom of repressed feelings. Doing dominates Eights' behavior, supported by thinking, with repressed feeling. To grow, Eights need to balance the thinking, doing, and feeling centers. The most effective way to achieve this balance is to allow the truth within to rise to the surface, recognize it for what it really is, and then reconcile it. If we know where imbalance lies and try to correct it through awareness, we may further harm ourselves and increase the imbalance. This can occur if we think, "I need to be more feeling to balance myself, and then I will be seen as more spiritual and enlightened." This statement and many others is a trick of the ego; it is striving for something in order to appear to others as someone you are not. The key here is "striving." In spiritual practice, striving to be ourselves is contrary to the energy flow of the universe and natural unfolding. If we have to try to swim, we will not swim. If we have to try to dance, we will be half a step off because we are *trying* to do it rather than doing it.

Kathy Hurley and Theodorre Donson, in *Enneagram for the 21st Century, Discover Your Soul Potential* and other works, have detailed the process of balancing the three centers. Don Richard Riso and Russ Hudson also have done extensive research on these centers. For a more in-depth examination of this area, we highly recommend their works.

We revised the Hurley-Donson model slightly to correspond to the inner motivations of the types, especially those of the One and Seven. Our model is unique in that the Stress and Heart Points give all the Enneatypes opportunities for growth in the repressed and supporting areas of the three centers. For example, for the Eight (as mentioned above) doing is dominant, thinking supports doing, and feeling is repressed. Eights move to the Heart Point of Two, at which they experience enhanced feeling (the dominant center for Twos). At the Stress Point of Five, Eights experience enhanced feeling through the supportive feeling center of Fives.

Center Balancing

Type	Centers: Dominant/Supportive /Repressed	Heart Point: Dominant/ Supportive	Stress Point: Dominant/ Supportive
1	Think/Do/Feel	Seven: Do/Feel	Four: Feel/Think
2	Feel/Do/Think	Four: Feel/Think	Eight: Do/Think
3	Do/Think/Feel	Six: Feel/Do	Nine: Feel/Think
4	Feel/Think/Do	One: Think/Do	Two: Feel/Do
5	Think/Feel/Do	Eight: Do/Think	Seven: Do/Feel
6	Feel/Do/Think	Nine: Feel/Think	Three: Do/Think
7	Do/Feel/Think	Five: Think/Feel	One: Think/Do
8	Do/Think/Feel	Two: Feel/Do	Five: Think/Feel
9	Feel/Think/Do	Three: Do/Think	Six: Feel/Do

In the above table, it is important to note that every repressed center in each Enneatype is experienced at the Heart and Stress Points, and thus provides opportunities for growth. Assertive types (One, Three, and Eight) repress feeling, Compliant types (Two, Six, and Seven) repress thinking, and Withdrawn types (Four, Five, and Nine) repress doing.

For personal and spiritual growth, it is essential to balance all three centers internally. When our energy is stuck in an ego fixation, the centers go out of balance, skewed toward the Enneatype. At that point, truth is repressed—hidden, but not lost. It will always rise to the surface as distorted, filtered, and deluded experiences.

Repressed Center, Hornevian Groups, and Triads

Type	Repressed Center	Hornevian Group	Triad
One	Feeling	Assertive	Body - Instinctual
Two	Thinking	Compliant	Heart - Feeling
Three	Feeling	Assertive	Heart – Feeling
Four	Doing	Withdrawn	Heart – Feeling
Five	Doing	Withdrawn	Head – Thinking
Six	Thinking	Compliant	Head – Thinking
Seven	Thinking	Compliant	Head – Thinking
Eight	Feeling	Assertive	Body - Instinctual
Nine	Doing	Withdrawn	Body - Instinctual

Instinctual Subtypes

There are three instinctual subtypes within all Enneatypes: the Self-Preservation subtype, Social subtype, and Sexual (One-to-One) subtype. Every person in each Enneatype manifests one of these subtypes as dominant over the others. For example, if the Eight is a self-preservationist, he is more interested in survival than in social or one-on-one relationships. His life revolves around making himself comfortable in his home environment, and he prefers to be left alone in his domestic life. If the Eight is a social type, he is more interested in interpersonal relationships rather than his home life or one–to-one relationships. If he is a One-to-One type, he is more interested in intimate, close relationships than in his home life or social, interpersonal relationships.

It is important to understand the instinctual motivation of ourselves and the people with whom we associate. For example, if an Eight is a self-preservationist and has a meaningful relationship with a Five who is a One-to-One subtype, the Eight will be more interested in his home life and survival while the Five will be more interested in a close, intimate relationship with the Eight. She will want to share her innermost secrets, look closely into her partner's eyes, and spend time alone with him. The Eight will want time alone, but not necessarily with the Five. The Eight will work hard to build a home for the Five and the rest of the family, looking at the future for survival. This couple may not survive if each member does not recognize and understand their partner's motivations.

Below is a brief description of the instinctual subtypes contained in all Enneatypes:

Self-Preservation: These people are more interested in building a nest, a home environment that will meet current and (more importantly) future needs. They focus on basic needs: food, shelter, and comfort. They tend to be loners within their types and are hard workers, looking to earn enough to survive. Worrying about where their next meal may come from, they lose sight of their significant relationships and social responsibilities.

Social: Social types are more interested in interpersonal relationships, and love to socialize within their Enneatype parameters. They focus on social concerns, groups, and mutual interests. They want to be accepted and place emphasis on social interactions, but lose focus on one-to-one relationships and self-preservation instincts.

Sexual (One-to-One): These people are more interested in close, intimate relationships in which each person shares his or her innermost secrets. They love time alone with their significant other, creating intense experiences. They love to lose themselves in their partners, merging in oneness, and lose focus on self-preservation instincts and social responsibilities. In a way, they are loners as long as they are alone with their significant other.

6 Enneatype One: The Perfectionist

AKA: Teacher, Crusader, Moralist, Reformer, Fundamentalist, Preacher
Caricatures: Felix Unger (from the movie and TV show, "The Odd Couple") Mary Poppins (from the movie, "Mary Poppins") George Bailey (from the movie, "It's a Wonderful Life")
Fixation / Passion: Anger / Resentment
Speech Pattern: Preach and teach
Basic Need: Perfection, to be good
Worst Fear: Being bad, defective, or evil
Mottos: Practice makes perfect.
>Rules are meant to be obeyed.
>If it ain't broke, don't fix it.

Spirituality – Lost or Given away: Perfection
Projected Mirrors: Criticism / Judgment

Growing Up:

As children, Ones leaned to repress their emotions. "Good little boys and girls do not act like that," they were told. Repressing emotions results in internal rage and anger—anger at being separated from Essence. They developed resentment of the way life *is* contrasted to how they think it should be, thus their striving for relative perfection. Ones learned to show exterior calmness that led to their stance of rigidity, a righteous posture at times. They learned how to present themselves to the outside world: impeccable grooming, fastidious habits, compulsive cleaning, and so on. Internally, the repression of anger leads to rage and resentment, resulting in a **severe inner critic.** Ones are constantly bombarded with internal criticism that tells them what is right and wrong based on relative perfectionism.

Ones grew up early in life; they had to become young men and women sooner than others. They developed a sense of seriousness because they had to show external control of their emotions, and they repressed childhood needs for play and fun.

Ones learned the rules...many times. They make rules based on their views of morals and rightness. Ones adhere to rules and expect everyone else to do the same: "Rules are meant to be obeyed" and "This is the company policy. There are no exceptions." Mastering the rules, Ones seek love and approval for being the "good boy/girl."

General Traits:

Ones will tell you what is right and wrong. They view the world as black and white, with little gray. Ones stick to procedures, are very conservative, and resist change. "If this is right, why change?" they may say. "It has worked for years." Knowing what is right and wrong, Ones project moralistic traits, which makes them appear highly moral and ethical in relative ways. They will tell you what is moral and ethical to the point of preaching. In fact, they are often known to preach and teach, which is their verbal style. By projecting morals, righteousness, and ethics outwardly, they find outlets to vent their internal anger and rage. They love to correct others and are often known as the champions of causes.

Enneatype Ones' internal critic makes them highly critical of themselves and other people. This creates self-denial of the things that would bring joy to them, and resentment is created because they are not enjoying life in the way they expected. The internal critic is relentless; their self-criticism projects outwardly as self-defense, and they become critical of others.

Ironically, Ones cannot handle external criticism. Why should they? They already know what perfect is, and are striving to live to those standards. External criticism opens wounds and exposes the "imperfect" world they have created. Spending enormous amounts of time and energy developing relative perfectionism, they anchor or dig in to their set ways. They are afraid to make decisions based on things other than what they have developed in perfectionism because they are afraid to make mistakes. They like to think things over for a while and consider all the options, to the point of procrastination. They are slow, methodical, and ponderous when it comes to open-ended options, and will painstakingly research every option before making a decision. Once they have decided, they will resist changing decisions because, "I have done all of the research, and this is the right way."

Ones are so concerned about how they appear, and strive for love based on the external presentation of the "good boy/girl", that they are cognizant of what others think about them. "What will my parents [or the neighbors] say?" is a typical concern.

Because Ones are so critical and detailed, they make good accountants, policy and procedure writers, ministers, and house cleaners. When Ones are asked to vacuum carpets, they move all the furniture in every room and make sure they clean the entire carpet, every inch. Ones often are obsessive–compulsive personalities.

The defense mechanism used by Ones is reaction formation: doing something positive to overcome something thought of as negative. For example, Ones may think about hatred, but since they consider it to be negative, they push it out of their consciousness and try to replace it with positive thoughts, such as love. They think of "hatred" as bad and "love" as good. However, repression of thoughts and feeling may develop into aberrant thinking and behavior patterns. Ones may use the reverse of the example and moralize, while personally they act immorally.

Wing Subtypes:

As the movement of energy flows through the Enneagram, we are not limited to one type of behavior that puts us into predefined boxes. As ego increases its control over us, we tend to fixate at a specific type or aspect of the Enneagram. As ego relinquishes control and the self-actualized personality emerges, energy flows move us constantly as we develop strategies for life based on higher states of the Enneagram. These may be known as holy ideas, virtuous flow, and etcetera.

The energy flows allow us to move to one of the adjacent Enneatypes, which are called the Wing subtypes. Although it is more common for most people to live on one of the Wing subtypes, we have found that the more self-actualized a person is, the fewer behavioral patterns develop at one subtype. Many of the people we know exhibit behavior that is balanced between the two subtypes of the main Enneatype.

The One at the Nine - Ones, as well as Nines, are Body-based or Instinctual types. Nines are known for their ability to see all sides of the story, and tend to assign everything equal importance. Ones are critical, detailed, and self-righteous. Nines fixate on sloth, Ones on anger. Nines need peace and harmony and Ones need perfection. Ones at the Nine are very critical and detailed, and they can see all sides. They may prolong decision making more than either Enneatype individually. Integrating the intuition of the Nine, the One at Nine can grow by reflecting on discerning energies that arise. Since both of these types are introverted on the surface, One at Nine will generally remain introverted even under the surface. However, Ones at Nine can loosen up through the humor instinct of the Nine and have a little fun. They will tend to be more sarcastic than the typical Nine. People in this subtype include Al Gore.

The One at the Two – Ones are Body-based or Instinctual types whereas; Twos are Heart or

Feeling types. Twos are known to be kind, generous, outgoing, and giving to others. They need others to need them. Ones are critical, detailed, and self-righteous. Twos fixate on pride, Ones on anger. Twos need to be of service to others and Ones need perfection. Ones at Two are more outgoing than Ones or the Ones at Nine. Outgoing Ones will drive their causes and righteousness home, even to the extent of heated debates. Like Twos, Ones at Two vocalize their criticism of others, especially when scorned. They can be highly active and aggressive. Like Twos, Ones at Two can be compassionate and empathetic, which matches their ethical and moral standards. Ones at Two can grow through compassion and empathy, especially when they allow these virtues to rise to the surface. People in this subtype include Ralph Nader and Jane Fonda.

Path of Integration (Heart Points):

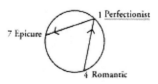

Ones move to Seven when relaxed; they have fun in life. Usually Ones are rigid and proper. When relaxed, they loosen up and enjoy life more, easing their inner critics. They lose their compulsive fastidiousness and become more spontaneous and less organized and time-conscious. They may fear losing control of themselves, a fear that may drop them back to the One Enneatype. True growth will allow the One to continue energy movement at the Seven and forward through the other Integration Paths.

Path of Disintegration (Stress Points):

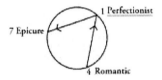

When experiencing undue stress, Ones move to Four. Overburdened by their incessant striving for relative perfection, and feeling that no one appreciates them, they start to fantasize and daydream of what they do not have that others have: "Why do other people get away with things and I do not? How come I am the only one who is responsible? Why do I pay the price and others do not?" At the Four, Ones often burst out of their self-control and become emotional as anger and resentment arise. In the move to Four, Ones may further deteriorate and use their growing anger to be "bad little boys or girls." They may become self-indulgent, thinking that they have earned it, and blame others for their anger and aberrant behavior: "You made me get angry!"

When the anger arises internally, Ones can recognize the source. It is the anger of not being allowed to be who they truly are...having to fit other people's definition of "good"... selling themselves out to fit others' ideas of perfection...listening to the omnipresent critical internal voice (that actually sounds like someone else)...and never thinking they are good enough. As truth is reconciled, Ones may experience positive traits of the Four: creativity and deep feeling. In letting go, Ones are propelled back to the One position, plus automatically move to the Heart Point, Path of Integration of the Seven as they integrate themselves. At the Seven, Ones have fun and can experience life without being tense. They see that there are other possibilities associated with perfection and that perfection is not limited to what they think.

Levels of Evolution:

Unevolved Ones can be dogmatic, self-righteous, intolerant, and rigid. Knowing perfection, they push their perfectionistic tendencies on others and deal in absolutes: they know the truth and if you want salvation, this is the only way to it. Perfectionism drives their critical natures, especially toward other people. At very unhealthy levels, the repressed rage rises to the surface, driving aberrant compulsive behavior, and they do the opposite of what they preach because they lose control of internal emotions. They become condemnatory, punitive, and cruel.

Average Evolved Ones become idealists and feel it is up to them to improve everything. They are reformers, advocates, critics, and crusaders, aligning themselves with those who share their perfectionistic ways and causes. They are afraid to make mistakes, which causes them to procrastinate. They become orderly and well organized, usually maintaining daily schedules and "things to do" lists, and experience stress when these lists are not completed. They become impersonal, rigid, and logical, and can be self-righteous and obsessed with time and punctuality. They are impatient, compulsive about tasks to the point of fastidiousness, and do not settle for anything less than what they consider perfection. Seeing other people get away with things by bending rules, Ones become indignant and resentful.

Evolved Ones do what they say they are going to do and live up to their own standards. They are genuine; people can trust their integrity. They are spontaneous, know how to enjoy life, and practice non-judgment because their inner critics have been silenced. They achieve unconditional love.

7 Enneatype Two: The Giver

AKA: Helper, Caretaker, Enabler, Friend
Caricatures: Edith Bunker (from the TV show, "All in the Family) Carmella Soprano (from the TV show, "The Sopranos) Mary Bailey (from the movie, "It's a Wonderful Life")
Fixation / Passion: Pride / Flattery
Speech Pattern: Hysterics, flattery
Basic Need: To be needed, to be of service, to help
Worst Fear: Being unloved or unneeded
Mottos: A friend in need is a friend indeed.
            What would people do without me?
            How can I help?
Spirituality – Lost or Given Away: Self-worth
Projected Mirrors: Neediness

Growing Up:

As children, Twos learned that to get attention and love, they had to give to others through service and flattery. But giving to others to get attention or love causes us to set aside our own needs, which leads to delusional thoughts that other people need us while we do not need them. This attitude results in pride. Giving to others so they will need us means that love will not be given for being ourselves—we have to trade giving to in order to receive. True giving is not expecting anything in return, but Twos expect love in return for giving. Love in these cases is conditional, thus not real love. Pride is inflated self-worth; it depends upon the approval of others. When we live for the approval of others, we become their prisoners. As we seek more approval, we fall deeper into desperate isolation and imprisonment. Thinking they do not need help because they are the helpers, Twos develop intense pride. How can you help others if you cannot help yourself?

Twos learned to flatter. They want to feel that they are the most important people in the lives of others. As children, flattery of parent, siblings, relatives, and other people gained Twos attention that they equated with love.

General Traits:

Twos have the ability to please even the most difficult people. They learned to shut themselves down and do whatever was required to satisfy others, which is like trying to please the most difficult father or mother. Masking their true nature, catering to others, Twos lose their true selves in their striving for approval. They fear rejection, believing that rejection equals worthlessness. When we depend on others for our self-worth, we are in trouble! Feeling worthless, Twos become assertive and lash out at other people, reminding them, "See all the things I do for you? Where would you be without me? I scratch your back; you need to scratch mine."

Twos are attracted to people on their way up socially. They like to be in the background promoting people who are close to them and who give them the attention they crave. They can be social butterflies, hosting parties attended by the "who's who." When Twos walk into a room full of people, they think, "There are people here who need my help."

Twos who associate with many people find themselves altering their personality for each person to satisfy the many diverse needs of others. This causes them to develop a sense of many false selves: "Which one of these people is me?" Twos define themselves through others, yet they crave freedom and feel confined by other people, especially when they do not receive responses from them. Twos need intimacy.

Twos, sensing being not needed, will do anything, including manipulation, to get attention. They negate others' boundaries, thinking they are responding to needs. Ironically, as Twos push out to get others to need them, they tend to push them away, intensifying their feelings of worthlessness. Twos will disintegrate until they cater to their own needs.

The defense mechanism of Twos is repression—they repress anything that does not match their image of themselves. Twos defend their actions by saying, "What is the problem? I am giving myself to others. Others need me, and my actions are justified because they do need my help."

Professionally, Twos do well in service professions such as doctor, nurse, counselor, and nun.

Wing Subtypes:

As the movement of energy flows through the Enneagram, we are not limited to one type of behavior that puts us into predefined boxes. As ego increases its control over us, we tend to fixate at a specific type or aspect of the Enneagram. As ego relinquishes control and the self-actualized personality emerges, energy flows move us constantly as we develop strategies for life based on higher states of the Enneagram. These may be known as holy ideas, virtuous flow, and etcetera.

The energy flows allow us to move to one of the adjacent Enneatypes, which are called the Wing subtypes. Although it is more common for most people to live on one of the Wing subtypes, we have found that the more self-actualized a person is, the fewer behavioral patterns develop at one subtype. Many of the people we know exhibit behavior that is balanced between the two subtypes of the main Enneatype.

The Two at the One - Twos are Heart or Feeling types, whereas Ones are Body-based or Instinctual types. Ones are critical, detailed, and self-righteous. Twos are kind, generous, outgoing, and giving. Ones fixate on anger, Twos on pride. Ones seek perfection, and Twos need to be of service to others. Twos at One are serious with purpose like the One, and warm, loving, caring and outgoing like the Two. They focus on service to others, preferring to stay in the background, and tend to be emotionally restrained like Ones. They can be so much of service to others that they struggle for a sense of self. People in this subtype include Florence Nightingale and Mother Teresa.

The Two at the Three – Twos, like Threes, are Heart -based or Feeling types. Threes are known for their accomplishments. They are the Type A, American corporate ideal personalities focused on self-promotion. Twos are warm, outgoing, and caring toward other people. Threes fixate on vanity, Twos on pride. Threes need to be accepted for their accomplishments, and Twos need to be needed by others. Twos at Three are very outgoing, like both Twos and Threes. They crave to network with other people and organize their lives to be around others as much as possible. Twos at Three are ambitious like the Three and caring and warm like the Two, which results in a façade that can be very agreeable to other people. Threes do not show the caring that Twos express and can be seen as shallow, but with the Two's warm exterior, this combination gives an impression of genuineness. People in this subtype include Regis Philbin and Merv Griffin.

Path of Integration (Heart Points):

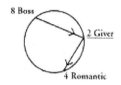

Twos move to Four when relaxed. Like Fours, Twos withdraw into themselves and reflect on their needs and feelings. As feelings arise at Four, Twos realize the traps they created pleasing others rather than themselves. They recognize their own needs and concentrate on meeting them. By meeting their own needs, they find that helping others is blessed when they do not expect anything in return. They no longer strive to be needed.

Path of Disintegration (Stress Points):

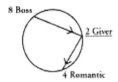

When experiencing undue stress, Twos move to Eight. Sensing that people do not appreciate the things they do for them, and that people may abandon them and do not need their help, Twos reveal toughness at Eight. They may challenge those around them whom they blame for the stress by being confrontational like the Eight. They can be aggressive and strong. They may threaten others with abandonment or major lawsuits. If they continue to deteriorate at the Eight, Twos will push away their loved ones and experience abandonment themselves.

They will get what they fear most: people do not need them.

When their pride is hurt, Twos can notice the feeling internally and allow the source of the hurt to surface so they can see it and reconcile the energy associated with it. They may recognize hurt pride in rarely feeling they are allowed to be themselves and have their own needs met, frequently catering to others for the recognition and love that they already possess, and feeling inadequate to meet their own needs internally. As the truth is revealed and reconciled, Twos may experience positive traits of the Eight: taking care of themselves and feeling independent. In letting go of pride, Twos are propelled back to the Two point, plus automatically move to the Heart Point Path of Integration at the Four. They experience authentic feelings of creativity and selfishness. (Selfishness is not necessarily negative as many of us may think. At this level, it can be very positive to take care of oneself.)

Levels of Evolution:

Unevolved Twos have a need to be needed by others that is so overwhelming, they may manipulate and undermine other people. They use guilt to get what they want: "See what I do for you? Where would you be if it were not for me?" They seek to dominate and coerce others to get what they want. Unevolved Twos rationalize their behavior by playing the victim and claiming abuse. Trying to ease pain of rejection, they may overeat or use drugs.

Average evolved Twos can be very seductive, friendly, and full of good intentions for helping others; however, they tend to talk about it more than do it. Twos chatter away constantly about their relationships and the things they do for other people. To obtain approval, they use flattery, seduction, caresses, and other devices. Striving for intimacy, they meddle, smother, and are overly possessive. "I am doing this for your own good. I know what is best for you." They can exhaust themselves trying to help others, and can be so needy that they become martyrs. Other people may feel very uncomfortable around them.

Evolved Twos live the virtues of compassion and empathy. They are genuinely caring, warm, and loving people who give to others, expecting nothing in return. They realize that the gift of giving is in the giving. They take care of themselves and achieve unconditional love.

8 Enneatype Three: The Performer

AKA: Achiever, CEO, Motivator
Caricatures: Willy Loman (from the play, "Death of a Salesman") Richard Fish (from the TV show, "Ally McBeal") Charles Foster Kane (from the movie, "Citizen Kane")
Fixation / Passion: Vanity / Deceit
Speech Pattern: Self-promotion: "I am the best."
Basic Need: Efficiency, acceptance, and desirability
Worst Fear: Being worthless and unable to accomplish things
Mottos: "My work is never done."
         "Fake it until you make it."
         "Appearances are everything."
Spirituality – Lost or Given Away: Authenticity
Projected Mirrors: Striving

Growing Up:

As children, Threes learned that they received attention by achieving, and the more they achieved the more attention they got. Threes developed efficiency so they could accomplish more in the same amount of time, and habitually stayed busy and productive. Threes were not valued for who they were, and learned to mimic success through achievements. They felt they had to pretend to be someone else, thus Threes learned to deceive the people around them so that others did not know who they really were dealing with. Being well known and identified with achievements does not satisfy the internal needs of Threes. In order to present the façade of success, Threes repress their real feelings and real identities, believing they are whom they project. They learned that there is no room for feelings in achievements.

As children, Threes learn to project images that attain the widest approval. They do not want to appear unsuccessful, because this would cause feelings of being unworthy coupled with shame.

General Traits:

The lives of Threes revolve around work, achievements, and success. Threes are impatient with the natural unfolding and energy flow of the universe, and hope to make things happen within their timeframes. Placing hope in their work, ignoring the natural energy flow, Threes develop the fixation of vanity. Vanity puts personal achievement above all else. It says, "I am the best. I control my own destiny. I am great and need no one, including the Creator." They feel they are pseudo-gods or demigods.

Threes are the American corporate ideal—Type A personalities with a burning desire for success. Success for Threes means practicing the attention-getting strategies they learned as children. This may mean they must be the best swimmer in the Olympics, the best monk at the monastery, or the best chief executive officer of a large company. They not only want to succeed, they want to look good doing it. The need to looking good at being successful is similar to the Two's desire to be needed by others; both create a prison-like atmosphere. Corporate America (which has a Three personality itself) thrives on competition, and Threes fit right in. They are effective leaders who want to be loved for their achievements rather than for who they are. In fact, they do not know who they are because they identify themselves with their "press clippings." The internal drives of Threes become frantic if Threes think they are on a road to failure, because they feel they cannot let others see them fail. Doing so would create feelings of rejection, unworthiness, and shame.

Networking with other people is a plus for Threes because they are charismatic and appear to show genuine concern for those they interact with. Beneath the surface, however, Threes are self-promoting and do not really care about what other people feel. Therefore, Threes do not usually associate with people who cannot help them achieve their career objectives. They are "smoke and mirrors" types who deceive others into thinking they care. Threes are more interested in working by themselves than on teams; they think they are more efficient that way and can control the frantic pace and successful outcomes. They will stay within rules and procedures as long as the rules and procedures do not hinder their chances for success.

Threes are "fake it until you make it" types. Below the surface they do not have it all together. They are insecure and avoid intimate relationships, which require depth and honesty. Typically, Threes mask their real selves. Significant relationships with

Threes are usually those of convenience and image, such as keeping a "trophy wife / husband" to assist them in their pursuit of achievements.

Threes use self-promotion as a defense mechanism. They focus on their accomplishments and make sure other people know how valuable they are. They are extremely image conscious and can change their images at will to obtain the most approval.

Professionally, Threes make good salespeople, advertising executives, and chief executive officers. They excel in areas in which image and presentation are important.

Wing Subtypes:

As the movement of energy flows through the Enneagram, we are not limited to one type of behavior that puts us into predefined boxes. As ego increases its control over us, we tend to fixate at a specific type or aspect of the Enneagram. As ego relinquishes control and the self-actualized personality emerges, energy flows move us constantly as we develop strategies for life based on higher states of the Enneagram. These may be known as holy ideas, virtuous flow, and etcetera.

The energy flows allow us to move to one of the adjacent Enneatypes, which are called the Wing subtypes. Although it is more common for most people to live on one of the Wing subtypes, we have found that the more self-actualized a person is, the fewer behavioral patterns develop at one subtype. Many of the people we know exhibit behavior that is balanced between the two subtypes of the main Enneatype.

The Three at the Two – Twos, as well as Threes, are Heart-based Feeling types. Twos are known to be kind and generous, outgoing, and giving to others. Threes are hard driving; Type A personalities that thrive on achievements and careers. Twos fixate on pride, Threes on vanity. Twos need to be of service to others, and Threes need to achieve success and look good while doing it. Threes at Two can be helpful like Twos and also maintain the poise and self-confidence of Threes. They are more outgoing and spontaneous than the other subtype. They need to be accepted like Twos, and have the ability to slickly deceive others. This subtype includes John Travolta and Bill Clinton.

The Three at the Four – Fours, as well as Threes, are Heart-based Feeling types. Fours are introverted, withdrawn, perfectionists, emotional, and moody. Threes are extroverted, assertive, and repress their feelings and emotions. They avoid feelings, thinking feelings are not necessary for success. Fours fixate on envy, Threes on vanity. Fours need to feel special and unique, and Threes need approval from other people to convince then they are successful. Threes at Four are serious and moody performers. They strive for perfection in their achievements and have high professional integrity. They tend to combine the self-doubt of the Four with the achievement and efficiency of the Three. This subtype includes Oprah Winfrey and Madonna.

Path of Integration (Heart Points):

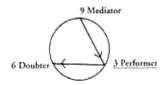

Threes move to Six when relaxed. They become more interested in working with a team rather than by themselves, as most Threes prefer. Being more of a team player, Threes commit to the goals of others and will become more intimate in relationships. Threes have a tendency to rush in achieving their goals; they are fast and efficient workers. Speed and efficiency preoccupies Threes and keeps them from going within themselves. At the Heart Point of Six, they slow down; this gives them time to reflect on their real feelings. Finding their feelings, Threes can grow in compassion and empathy.

Path of Disintegration (Stress Points):

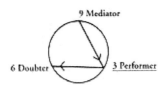

When experiencing undue stress, Threes move to Nine. Questioning their value in the world, they may think there is no true happiness in achievements. They may notice the elation of an accomplishment, but soon the elation wears off, and they need more and more as they relentlessly pursue love through achievements and recognition. They become disillusioned, and if they continue to deteriorate, will zone out and become apathetic, accomplishing nothing and living their worst fear: being worthless.

At this low point, Threes who observe their inner realities look for the cause of the disillusionment. They may find it in the deceit they present to the world and to themselves. They may realize the truth of the pain in feeling they are not allowed to be themselves and must constantly do or accomplish things—that they are not good enough, and must relentlessly pursue unattainable goals. As truth is revealed and reconciled, Threes may experience positive traits of the Nine: they connect with themselves and their feelings. Realizing they do not have to accomplish anything to be worthwhile, they let go of vanity and deceit. They are propelled back to the Three point, plus automatically move to the Heart Point, Path of Integration at the Six. They experience being a team player and having loyalty to coworkers, friends, and family. The Threes now are able to commit to goals and people with a commitment that is genuine and not self-promoting. They present themselves as themselves, not as what they think other people want to see.

Levels of Evolution:

Unevolved Threes can lie, cheat, and steal to be the best, to be successful. They fear failure and the shame that comes with it. They speed up, relentlessly pursuing their goals at any cost. At the lower levels, they cover up mistakes and can become psychopathic. Ironically, doing anything to get attention and look good actually makes them look bad, and they get what they fear most: failure.

Average evolved Threes are achievement-, career-, and goal-oriented. They want other people to notice them through their achievements, and identify themselves with their careers. They have intimacy problems because they know how to package themselves, and will change to become what others expect of them (as long as the others can help their careers). They constantly tell others about their achievements, promoting themselves and hoping for more recognition. They are narcissistic and pretentious, and can be hostile and contemptuous to people and bureaucratic structures that hinder their careers.

Evolved Threes are self-accepting, integrated with their feelings, and have compassion and empathy for others. They are genuine and caring, and present themselves as who they are, not what they achieve.

9 Enneatype Four: The Romantic

AKA: Artist, Tragic Romantic, Victim, Unique Person
Caricature: Blanche DuBois (from the play and movie, "A Streetcar Named Desire") Ally McBeal (from the TV show, "Ally McBeal") Livia Soprano (from the TV show, "The Sopranos") Cyrano de Bergerac (from the play, "Cyrano de Bergerac")
Fixation / Passion: Envy / Melancholy
Speech Pattern: Melodramatic, melancholic dialogue
Basic Need: Being unique and special
Worst Fear: Being insignificant, without identity
Mottos: "No one understands me."
       "How can people be so happy—my world is
          falling apart!"
       "Romeo, Romeo, wherefore art thou, Romeo?"
Spirituality – Lost or Given Away: Soul connection to Source
Projected Mirrors: Special / Unique

Growing Up:

As children, Fours felt abandoned. Initially, abandonment manifested through a deep sense of loss of connection to Source. This resulted in loneliness, and augmented their sense of abandonment from other people. Feeling melancholy, or a deep sadness, stems from the perception of the loss of love from being disconnected from the Creator or the universe. Feelings of separation—of being special or unique—arise. They feel, "How can I be safe when God has abandoned me?" or "I would not have been abandoned if I were worthy."

Four children withdraw and look within for connection. They strive for relationships that fill deep emotional holes. In addition to the human sense of abandonment from Source, Fours experience a feeling of abandonment from their fathers, mothers, and siblings, which intensifies their emotional swings. Four children, unwilling to experience the totality of emotion generated in the loss, withdraw further. Withdrawal creates emotional disconnection from people in an attempt to avoid pain, and it supports internal dreaming and romantic fanaticizing (looking for the knight on the white horse for rescue).

When Four children look outward, they see other people as happy. Fours are not happy, thus envy arises. They feel, "How can they be happy, when my whole world is falling apart?" "Why can't I be happy?" "I can only be happy when someone accepts me for who I am."

Four children may think they were switched in the hospital, that their parents are not their real parents, or that UFOs brought them to earth.

General Traits:

Fours, though withdrawn, need to be around other people. They crave dramatic relationships, love emotional highs and lows, and get bored with mainstream ordinariness. They feel that living life means to tread upon the emotional extremes.

Boredom drives Fours into internal fantasies that generate outward emotional responses, because they confuse the real world with their imaginary ones. Most Fours feel that their inner worlds are more exciting than the outer world of reality.

Fours search for that one person who will save them and accept them for their uniqueness. They want to be rescued. Ironically, when someone comes along who wants to rescue them, Fours tend to push the person away because either they feel flawed and unworthy of rescue, or they think the person must be flawed to want them. Fours reject the would-be rescuer before he or she has a chance to abandon them.

Internally, Fours' romantic fantasies are what they seek; however, fantasies are only fantasies. Fours love from afar. When significant people are away from them, they pine for them to be closer. Being closer initiates the push-away pattern of not being good enough for love. This dance of push-pull patterns is relentless.

As envy arises, Fours are attracted to what is missing, like a little girl looking for a father figure to replace the real father who abandoned her when she was four. They focus on what other people have that they do not have. Envy can drive Fours to dramatic emotional displays; they are drama kings and queens. Envy drives Fours to destruct what is good in others: "If I can't have it, no one will."

Thinking they are flawed, and masking internal shame, Fours project external uniqueness. They show emotions, manners, idiosyncratic tendencies, eccentricities, special perfectionism bordering on exotic, and a taste for peculiar luxuries such as odd art and unique collections. Fours can be incredibly artistic, mastering music, drawing, sculpture, and writing. Their imaginations drive these unique art forms.

The defense mechanism of Fours is introjections. Fours fantasize about their special "knight" who will come along and rescue them and love them for their uniqueness. This is the desire to look outwardly for love that was fantasized because it is easier and more desirable than loving yourself.

Professionally, Fours make good graphic artists, sculptors, musicians, and writers, and often excel in areas where introspection and fantasy are important.

Wing Subtypes:

As the movement of energy flows through the Enneagram, we are not limited to one type of behavior that puts us into predefined boxes. As ego increases its control over us, we tend to fixate at a specific type or aspect of the Enneagram. As ego relinquishes control and the self-actualized personality emerges, energy flows move us constantly as we develop strategies for life based on higher states of the Enneagram. These may be known as holy ideas, virtuous flow, and etcetera.

The energy flows allow us to move to one of the adjacent Enneatypes, which are called the Wing subtypes. Although it is more common for most people to live on one of the Wing subtypes, we have found that the more self-actualized a person is, the fewer behavioral patterns develop at one subtype. Many of the people we know exhibit behavior that is balanced between the two subtypes of the main Enneatype.

The Four at the Three – Threes as well as Fours are Heart-based Feeling Types. Threes are known for their ambition, repressed feelings, and high external assertive energy. Fours are withdrawn, moody, and emotional. Threes fixate on vanity, Fours on envy. Threes need to be successful, and Fours need to feel special and unique. Fours at Three combine creativity and ambition. They are concerned with what other people think and love audiences; they can be great actors and actresses. They are more extroverted and more materialistic than the other subtype. The Four at Three can be narcissistic like the Three and emotionally grandiose like the Four. This subtype includes Judy Garland and Blanche DuBois.

The Four at the Five – Fives are Head-based Thinking types; Fours are Heart-based Feeling types. Fives are known for their accumulation of knowledge, while Fours are artistic and emotional. Fives disdain emotional displays. Both Fives and Fours are withdrawn types that like to be left alone and are highly imaginative. They combine the cerebral creativity and originality of the Five with the introspective emotions of the Four. Fours at Five are more into fantasy than the other subtype. Fives do not like external structures that limit their thinking and Fours do not like the mundane; therefore, Fours at Five can be antisocial and break rules. They are attracted to eccentric, far-out ideas and theories. This subtype includes Edgar Allan Poe and James Dean.

Path of Integration (Heart Points):

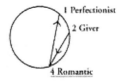

Fours move to One when relaxed. They learn to curtail their moods and become more disciplined, and can be very productive. Ones are very discerning, especially with the differentiation between fantasy and reality. Fours at the Heart Point of One learn that their internal fantasy world is different than external reality. They find value in themselves, cease looking for what is missing, and stop waiting to be rescued. They recognize values that were always present but repressed: connection with the universe, happiness, and strength.

Path of Disintegration (Stress Points):

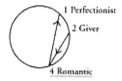

When experiencing undue stress, Fours move to Two. Realizing that their withdrawal from the world is causing undue tension, especially in the way they handle relationships in the push-pull style, they move to the Stress Point of Two. At the Two, they move out of their shells and romanticized fantasies to reality, striving to correct their loneliness by contrived friendliness. In deterioration, they may try too hard, even dramatizing melodramatically to find out if others love them. In this manner, they will drive away their significant others and thus will experience what they fear most: abandonment.

Fours who observe their behavior and allow the truth in the stress to arise may recognize its source, and then reconcile the energy associated with it. They may realize that other people do not have more than they do, Essence in the universe is omnipresent and never abandoned them, and that they are unique and special within themselves and do not need to be rescued. As truth is revealed and reconciled, Fours may experience positive traits of the Two: openness and deep caring for others, being grateful for what they have, and humility. In letting go of envy, Fours are propelled back to the Four point, plus automatically move to the Heart Point, Path of Integration at the One. Here they experience that who they are is good. They become productive and stop dramatizing and emoting.

Levels of Evolution:

Unevolved Fours are haunted by debilitating melancholy and sadness. Their self-worth declines when they realize their fantasies are not real and their dreams are not realized. They become paralyzed and delusional, with morbid thoughts edging toward suicide and self-mutilation. They hate themselves and fear that no one will rescue them, so they develop worldly hatred through envy. Unevolved Fours are like black holes; they will drain energy from others. The more energy you have, the more they will drain. They are sometimes known as "energy vampires."

Average evolved Fours dwell in artistic, uniquely romanticized lives. As withdrawn types, Fours reinforce their sense of self-worth through fantasy, especially romantic fantasy. They seek to be rescued. They are introverted, moody, emotional, and sometimes tragic. They love the highs and lows of emotion, feeling that normal is mundane and ordinary. Fours feel they are unique. They can be fastidious, impractical, and envious of others. Self-pity drives them internally, and they dwell on fantasy.

Evolved Fours realize that they are connected to the Creator and the universe. Their sense of abandonment wanes. They find themselves and their significance in the world. They live in objective reality, learning that the real world is beautiful and comforting. They find unconditional love for themselves and other people. Evolved fours can be very creative, inspired, and motivated to express themselves in productive, energetic ways.

10 Enneatype Five: The Observer

AKA: Expert, Thinker, Genius
Caricature: Mr. Spock and Data (both from the TV show, "Star Trek") Ebenezer Scrooge (from the movie, "A Christmas Carol")
Fixation / Passion: Avarice / Stinginess
Speech Pattern: Erudite, knowledgeable
Basic Need: Knowledge, capable, and competent
Worst Fear: Being incompetent, useless, and incapable
Mottos: "Knowledge is power."
　"Geniuses are rarely recognized in their own time."
　"First you buy books, and if any money is left over, you buy food."
Spirituality – Lost or Given Away: Intelligence
Projected Mirrors: Withdrawal

Growing Up:

As children, Fives found little or no privacy in their lives, possibly due to intrusive parents or siblings who invaded their space. They withdrew into their cerebral world to feel safe and avoid painful emotions. Five children learned that they were accepted and valued only for their knowledge, and they were coerced to earn the highest grades in school. They spent a lot of time on their own—reading, hiking, studying, playing, practicing some type of music appreciation, or thinking. Fives use a lot of energy thinking. Being withdrawn, they do not handle spontaneous reactions in social settings well because they need time to reflect and figure things out, which leads to a delay in doing. Therefore, they are greedy with the amount of energy they expend in the external world. Fives often lower their external needs in order to preserve privacy.

Five children learned that competency in life comes from the amount of knowledge one obtains. They seek to become an expert at something, even if the subject is obscure and has little relevance to the real world.

General Traits:

Fives are Head-based, Thinking people. They love to theorize, and strive for knowledge: "Knowledge is power." They feel that the more knowledge they acquire, the more competent they are. How much knowledge is enough? They are obsessed with knowledge accumulation and seldom think they have enough. Ironically, Fives do not accumulate knowledge; they accumulate information. Fives are analytical and logical. They avoid acting until they have all the information, thus doing is repressed.

Fives are observers in life, and believe that the observer has no effect on what is being observed. As they function, they take mental pictures and store them in their cerebral databases for analysis and future use. They usually are on the cutting edge of technology and have the latest gadgets for knowledge management and data storage, such as personal digital assistants (PDAs), Palm Pilots, and computers.

Because Fives are stingy with their energy, they tend to want closed-ended agreements. Events and plans in their lives need to be precise so they know what to expect and how much energy to expend. They get tired at parties where they have to react spontaneously with people. Afterwards they reflect on every transaction encountered, and plan how they will react in the future in similar situations.

The defense mechanism of Fives is compartmentalization. They separate everything they do—different types of friends and tasks, for instance. Compartmentalization allows Fives to break everything apart for analysis.

Fives have difficulty with relationships because they do not like involvement and would rather stay in the background. Intimacy requires involvement, especially emotionally. Fives shun emotions because emotions are not logical. When choosing to be intimate, Fives recognize that intimacy may result in painful emotions, thus they take their time to think about whether or not the person they will be close to is worth a lifetime of pain. They often feel drained by expectations and emotions in relationships.

Professionally, Fives make good technical analysts, accountants, teachers, and ministers. They tend to excel in areas that allow them to work on their own.

Wing Subtypes:

As the movement of energy flows through the Enneagram, we are not limited to one type of behavior that puts us into predefined boxes. As ego increases its control over us, we tend to fixate at a specific type or aspect of the Enneagram. As ego relinquishes control and the self-actualized personality emerges, energy flows move us constantly as we develop strategies for life based on higher states of the Enneagram. These may be known as holy ideas, virtuous flow, and etcetera.

The energy flows allow us to move to one of the adjacent Enneatypes, which are called the Wing subtypes. Although it is more common for most people to live on one of the Wing subtypes, we have found that the more self-actualized a person is, the fewer behavioral patterns develop at one subtype. Many of the people we know exhibit behavior that is balanced between the two subtypes of the main Enneatype.

The Five at the Four – Fours are Heart-based Feeling types; Fives are Head-based Thinking types. Fours are emotional, moody, introverted, withdrawn, and perfectionistic. Fives are reclusive, withdrawn, unemotional, and logical. Fours fixate on envy; Fives fixate on greed. Fours need to feel special and unique, and Fives need to feel competent by accumulating knowledge. Fives at Four are introspective and emotional. They combine the uniqueness of Fours and the thinking of Fives, and can express special knowledge with others.

Combining the withdrawal styles of Fours and Fives, Fives at Four are very private and lonely. They are the most introverted type of the Enneagram. Like Fours, Fives at Four tend to fantasize about obscure things and may get lost in cerebral realities. This subtype includes Stephen King and Tim Burton.

The Five at the Six – Sixes, as well as Fives, are Head-based Thinking types. Sixes are fearful, attracted to groups and group thoughts, well organized, and detailed. Fives are individualists who are organized and detail-oriented. Sixes fixate on fear, Fives on greed. Sixes need to feel supported and safe. Fives find safety in their heads. Fives at Six combine the group thinking and detail of the Six with the observation and obscure analysis of the Five. This subtype is very erudite and scientific, the most intellectual of all subtypes. Both Fives and Sixes focus on the outside world, Fives with observation and Sixes with safety. Fives at Six do not display emotions. This subtype includes Bill Gates and Stephen Hawking.

Path of Integration (Heart Points):

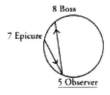

Fives move to Eight when relaxed. Eights are Body-based Instinctual types. Fives at Eight learn the instinctive traits of Eights, which aligns doing with their thoughts and feelings. They are more active and present at the Eight Heart Point. Eights are assertive types, and Fives at Eight are more forward with their energy. Fives energies at Eight flow more; they do not feel drained or greedy with their energies. They realize that they are not separate from reality, and that observing is connected to—and affects—objective reality.

Path of Disintegration (Stress Points):

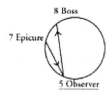

When experiencing undue stress, Fives move to Seven. Seeing that withdrawing into their inner sanctum is not working, their minds speed up and they move to the Seven. At the Stress Point of Seven, they can distract themselves with activity, albeit meaningless and scattered. They may become irritated, sarcastic, and insecure with their relationships. If the stress persists, they may increase activities, searching for stimulation. At this point, they may find that the meaningless chores and activities and the sarcasm expressed to loved ones will get them what they fear most: incompetence.

Fives are observers, and seeing themselves react at the Stress Point and allow truth to arise to be reconciled, they may find that being greedy with energy and time has shut them down to meaningful relationships...that they never lost the time and space they deserved...and that they already possess the knowledge they need to function and survive. As the truth is revealed and reconciled, Fives may experience positive traits of the Seven: spontaneity, outward energy, and fulfilling experiences—traits that are difficult for the Five to express. In letting go of avarice, Fives are propelled back to the Five point, plus automatically move to the Heart Point, Path of Integration at the Eight. Here they experience instinctual body energy creating an energy movement that feels strong, and they are present with their feelings and reactions.

Levels of Evolution:

Unevolved Fives fear the outside environment, thus they become isolated, eccentric, and reclusive. They feel worthless because they believe they do not possess the knowledge to survive in the world. They try to think their way through life. When they sense failure in thinking it through, they panic and may create cerebral, virtual "Loony Toons," hallucinating that the world is not as it is. Their minds go into overdrive, and they can fall into dark thoughts.

Average evolved Fives are intellectual, working out everything in their minds. They approach life logically and if something is not logical, they will try to figure it out. They practice what they will do and say at various functions and experiences, trying to think their feelings through. Like Ones, they may be rigid and artificial in their body movements. They love to observe and may (through observation) draw incorrect conclusions.

Evolved Fives find that they already possess the knowledge they need to live happily. They realize that they are not disconnected from life by observing it and they are part of all that occurs. Observation takes on a different twist. They feel connected to what they observe, and may have extraordinary insights about the world through observation. Evolved Fives find themselves. They learn to reconnect with their feelings and are compassionate and empathetic.

11 Enneatype Six: The Doubter

AKA: Trooper, Devil's Advocate, Cynic, Loyalist, Believer

Caricatures: Hamlet (phobic) (from the play, "Hamlet") Adolf Hitler (counter-phobic) Sherlock Holmes Barney Fife (from the TV show, "Mayberry RFD")

Fixation / Passion: Fear (Anxiety) / Cowardice

Speech Pattern: Team, "isms"

Basic Need: Security; to feel supported by external structures

Worst Fear: Unable to survive, with no support to cling to

Mottos: "Be careful out there."

"Whatever can go wrong, will go wrong."

"Why me?"

Spirituality – Lost or Given Away: Faith / Courage

Projected Mirrors: Cynicism

Growing Up:

As children, Sixes learned that the environment was not safe. They continually were bombarded with fear-based stimuli, lost faith that the Creator or universe would support them, and became doubters. They focused their attention on danger,

constantly looking around for the next peril that
would interfere with their safety.

Six children look for strong father figures—
people, who make them feel safe, someone to protect
them. The loss of the father figure triggers a feeling of
separation from the secure universal, essential
environment, and creates fear. Six children also may
have had mothers who were dominant and
overcompensated for weak fathers. This environment
tends to create fear, especially in boys who feel
overwhelmed by their mothers.

General Traits:

Sixes are team players, loyal to causes that
provide a sense of safety that Sixes feel they do not
possess. Sixes are in the Thinking triad, but repress
their thinking because they are seeking the security
they believe they lost. Thinking for Sixes involves
doubting their own thoughts and decisions. They
search for external means of feeling safe such as
corporations, the military, political affiliations, and
churches. This external security is delusional,
because Sixes tend to align themselves blindly. Once
they become loyal to causes or systems, they do not
want to be questioned about them. Sixes need the
apparent safety of these beliefs because beliefs are
the means Sixes think will take them back to
Essential losses.

Once Sixes adopt belief systems, they are
extremely loyal to them, fearing abandonment if they
do not prove themselves worthy to remain in the
system's safety. If Sixes think the belief system is

weakening, they may panic; creating paranoia that disturbs their superficial security. Even if the system does not weaken, if Sixes think it is deteriorating, they may sabotage it with their paranoia.

Sixes constantly scan the environment for danger. They are worst-case scenario (Murphy's Law) types, and usually are ready for worst cases because they focus their energy looking for them. At times they may resemble "deer in headlights" as they fear doing and making decisions, doubt their own thoughts. This fear leads to procrastination. When they decide to do something, they charge ahead like loyal soldiers, then—amazingly—retreat, as fear increases in the charge toward unknown landscapes. They are like balls bouncing back and forth, seeking external security in a perpetual phobic dance. Some Sixes are counter-phobic and try to prove there are no dangers by moving outwardly, performing dangerous stunts and risking their lives to show they are not afraid. This behavior pattern is known as the "Evel Knievel syndrome."

Sixes cannot stay still. Stressed, they walk around in circles with their heads down and shoulders hunched. They are filled with polarized thinking, and dualities arise: good bad, right wrong, this way or that way. This thinking keeps them in superficial motion, testing the waters to make sure the waters are warm and friendly. Unfortunately, inaction increases their fear. Phobic Sixes run, and counter-phobic Sixes charge.

Sixes are loyal to causes and systems. They do have many successes; however, because their minds are in overdrive, they forget their successes and concentrate on the failures: "Why did I fail? Wasn't I good enough?" Sixes are loyalists, but often question authority. They are especially keen at seeing inconsistencies and deceitful people, because that is where their energy is focused. ("Seek and ye shall find.") If you look for danger, you will find it.

Projection is the defense mechanism used by Sixes; they project their fears onto the outside world. They look for reasons why life is not going the way they think it should go, and project their dissatisfaction outwardly, looking for scapegoats and someone to blame.

Professionally, Sixes make good inspectors and quality assurance specialists. They excel at jobs that require troubleshooting, asking probing questions, and looking for inconsistencies.

Wing Subtypes:

As the movement of energy flows through the Enneagram, we are not limited to one type of behavior that puts us into predefined boxes. As ego increases its control over us, we tend to fixate at a specific type or aspect of the Enneagram. As ego relinquishes control and the self-actualized personality emerges, energy flows move us constantly as we develop strategies for life based on higher states of the Enneagram. These may be known as holy ideas, virtuous flow, and etcetera.

The energy flows allow us to move to one of the adjacent Enneatypes, which are called the Wing subtypes. Although it is more common for most people to live on one of the Wing subtypes, we have found that the more self-actualized a person is, the fewer behavioral patterns develop at one subtype. Many of the people we know exhibit behavior that is balanced between the two subtypes of the main Enneatype.

The Six at Five – Both Fives and Sixes are Head-based Thinking types. Fives are known for their technical expertise; they are knowledgeable and dedicate their lives to the accumulation of information. Sixes are detail-oriented, seeing inconsistencies and dualities. Fives fixate on greed, Sixes on fear. Fives need to think they are competent; Sixes need security and safety. Sixes at Five can be extremely good at problem solving, analyzing, and teaching, combining the knowledge of Fives and the questioning of Sixes. Fives are withdrawn types and Sixes are compliant types. Sixes at Five tend to be loners like Fives, and as loners do not look for outside advice. This subtype includes Mel Gibson and Richard Nixon.

The Six at Seven – Both Sevens and Sixes are Head-based Thinking types. Sevens are known for their frivolity, their ability to experience many pleasures in life. Sixes shun doing, fearful of making mistakes. Sevens fixate on gluttony, Sixes on fear. Sevens need to feel satisfied and happy; Sixes need to think they are safe. On the surface Sevens are assertive, charging ahead doing things they think will make them happy. Beneath the surface Sevens are compliant, wanting to go along with society as long as society lets them do what they want. Sixes are compliant types looking for security. Sixes at Seven are very sociable, funny, and serious people combining the social charms and graces of the Seven with the seriousness of the Six. Sixes and Sevens are procrastinators, and this subtype is no exception. They love to hang out with loved ones and friends, and enjoy sports and recreational activities. This subtype includes Tom Hanks and Meg Ryan.

Path of Integration (Heart Points):

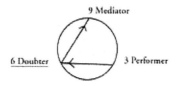

Sixes move to Nine when relaxed. Nines are Body-based Instinctual types. At Nine, Sixes' overactive thinking abates; they feel secure in their bodies. Like Nines, Sixes at Nine are peaceful and comfortable. They see goodness in the environment and stop looking for the dangers. Sixes will bounce back to the Six point when fears arise.

Path of Disintegration (Stress Points):

When experiencing undue stress, Sixes move to Three. When Sixes security comes crashing down, they panic and move to the Stress Point of Three. They become driven, work hard, and are concerned about the image they project. As they develop an intensified false image (deceit), they push harder for security, even to the extent of lying about their accomplishments. At this point, they may sabotage the structures around them with their increased phobias, and thus realize their greatest fear: insecurity.

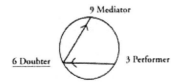

If Sixes can stop and observe fear arising, they can allow the source of the fear to surface and be reconciled. They may find that they were not allowed to be themselves and that the environment of the universe is safe. There is nothing to doubt or question, just relaxation of the chattering mind. As truth is revealed and reconciled, Sixes may experience positive traits of the Three: they feel a genuineness of self, and are productive and self-accepting. In letting go of fear, Sixes are propelled back to the Six point, plus automatically move to the Heart Point, Path of Integration at the Nine. Here they experience the positive traits of the Nine: an instinctual body energy that helps them ground and feels inner strength and balance. They become more present, and relax in the environment.

Levels of Evolution:

Unevolved Sixes can be paranoid, thinking that everyone is out to get them. Their minds go into overdrive as they search for safety and security. They feel worthless and insecure, and tend to cling and panic. They may stay in unhealthy relationships and jobs thinking, "The devil you know is better than the devil you don't know." They lash out at the beliefs and systems they thought would bring them security, and—ironically—sabotage these systems, further undermining their security bases. They finally achieve what they feared most: being left out and feeling insecure, with their entire world crashing down around them.

Average evolved Sixes seek security and safety in groups and beliefs. Being part of systems, they do not have to take responsibility for themselves. They follow the corporate image and spiel. They do not like to be pushed, as it disturbs their sense of security and makes them feel insecure. They may be passive-aggressive under pressure and tend to procrastinate, doubt, and act defensive.

Evolved Sixes stop looking for security outside themselves. They find peace within and learn to trust their instincts and inner guidance. Security and safety are within, not in the external world. Sixes reestablish their connection with Essence, the warm universal environment. Evolved Sixes are secure and grounded; they trust the environment, are lovable, and can be very charismatic. Self-actualized Sixes are trustworthy, reliable, trusting, courageous, positive, and compassionate.

12 Type Seven: The Epicure

AKA: Dilettante, Connoisseur, Generalist, Enthusiast
Caricatures: Peter Pan (from the movies, "Peter Pan" and "Hook") Alfie (from the movie, "Alfie") Scarlett O'Hara (from the book and movie, "Gone with the Wind") Auntie Mame (from the play and movie, "Mame")
Fixation / Passion: Gluttony / Planning
Speech Pattern: Quips
Basic Need: Idealism; to be happy and fulfilled
Worst Fear: Being deprived; having no activities that bring pleasure; internal pain
Mottos: "Variety is the spice of life."
   "Life is too short not to have fun."
   "You only live once—if you don't enjoy it, it's
      your own fault.")
Spirituality – Lost or Given Away: Nurturing
Projected Mirrors: Immaturity

Growing Up:

As children, Sevens learned to nurture themselves because the family nurturer (either their mother or father) was weak or not present. Sevens learned to occupy themselves and keep busy. They developed active minds. To avoid loneliness within, they look outwardly, experiencing life as if there was no tomorrow: "You will be dead forever. Life is for experiences." Unfortunately, Seven children learned that external activities numbed internal pain. As long as they stayed active, they avoided going within, and their spiritual growth was limited.

General Traits:

Sevens are Head-based Thinking types. Their thinking abilities, like those of Sixes, are repressed, utilized for incessant planning and avoiding inner reality. Sevens plan to give themselves many alternatives to enjoy life; they keep their options open. On weekends, they may plan to attend several events, knowing that they cannot attend all of them. They may try to attend them all, or go to those they think are most exciting, while keeping the other plans available in case the events are not what they expected. They usually attend events while the energy is high and leave before the energy wanes. The worst thing for Sevens is to be bored and have nothing to do. Sevens easily become bored, which is why they plan. Putting more on your plate than you can handle is gluttony—gluttony to the extent that one never experiences anything in depth, tasting but not digesting. No quantity of external activity is great enough to please a Seven.

Sevens are playful types; they want stimulation and seek peak experiences. Multiple experiences keep Sevens busy. By continually changing plans and activities, Sevens defend themselves, because it is difficult to hit a moving target. Doing a lot of things assures them that losing any one thing or friend will not hurt them.

Sevens seek happiness externally at any price. They are narcissistic, not thinking about anyone else as long as they get to experience. Rationalization is their primary defense mechanism: "We only live once. Life is to experience and enjoy, and if you do not enjoy it, it is your fault."

Sevens feel entitled—they expect certain things from life, and go for them. They expect people to like them and support their ideas. Sevens are very personable and fun to be with. They are charming like Twos, but when their charm does not work, fear and insecurity arise. They love spontaneity. Like Threes, Sevens are "fake it until you make it" types. Sevens and Threes are similar in many ways. The biggest difference is in their driving motivation: Threes want to be successful; Sevens want to have fun.

Since Sevens enjoy events and experiences with high energy levels, they most enjoy the beginning and planning stages of life and relationships because these are the higher energy stages. They tend to procrastinate with lesser energy parts of life, like sustaining relationships. Sevens fear and avoid intimacy because intimacy requires commitment and depth. They think commitment is limiting and boring, and avoid depth because they associate it with pain. Sevens prefer open-ended agreements rather than marriage: "You do your thing and I will do mine."

Sevens make good public relations people. They excel in jobs that do not require a lot of detail and offer a wide variety of experiences.

Wing Subtypes:

As the movement of energy flows through the Enneagram, we are not limited to one type of behavior that puts us into predefined boxes. As ego increases its control over us, we tend to fixate at a specific type or aspect of the Enneagram. As ego relinquishes control and the self-actualized personality emerges, energy flows move us constantly as we develop strategies for life based on higher states of the Enneagram. These may be known as holy ideas, virtuous flow, and etcetera.

The energy flows allow us to move to one of the adjacent Enneatypes, which are called the Wing subtypes. Although it is more common for most people to live on one of the Wing subtypes, we have found that the more self-actualized a person is, the fewer behavioral patterns develop at one subtype. Many of the people we know exhibit behavior that is balanced between the two subtypes of the main Enneatype.

The Seven at the Six – Both Sixes and Sevens are Head-based Thinking types. Sixes are detailed, doubting, and fearful. Sevens love to experience many things. Sixes fixate on fear, Sevens on gluttony. Sixes need security and safety; Sevens need to experience as much as they can. Sevens at Six are very positive in their outlook on life; they are funny and playful. On the low side, they can be manic and insecure. Otherwise, they are very productive and creative people. This subtype includes Robin Williams and Goldie Hawn.

The Seven at the Eight – Eights are Body-based Instinctual types, while Sevens are Head-based Thinking types. Eights are known for their strength and power. Sevens are frivolous and playful. Eights fixate on lust, Sevens on gluttony. Eights need truth and trust; Sevens need happiness. Sevens at Eight are materialistic. They are more into their bodies than basic Sevens, which makes them more grounded and practical. They combine the roughness of the Eight with the good nature of the Seven, and are good multi-taskers. This subtype includes Jack Nicholson and John F. Kennedy.

Path of Integration (Heart Points):

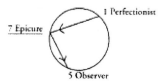

Sevens move to Five when relaxed. They become more introspective, slow down their minds, and focus on the quality rather than the quantity of experiences. They reconnect with Essence, realizing that true growth and happiness is within.

Path of Disintegration (Stress Points):

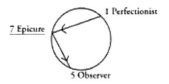

When experiencing undue stress, Sevens move to One. Feeling emptiness in their chaotic and scattered lifestyle and increasing boredom and unfulfilled goals, they tighten up and restrain themselves at the Stress Point of One. Bottling up their enthusiasm, Sevens at One become increasingly irritated, sarcastic, and nitpicking. They tend to preach, like the One. Deteriorating further, Sevens realize that pain still pursues them from within. They increase activity and panic, over-driving their minds to the point where they live their worst fear: being trapped in pain.

If Sevens can stop and observe the pain in deprivation, truth arises and they may realize that being oneself includes internal reality and feelings, that they were good enough and did not have to grow up too fast, and that things are not substitutes for happiness. Happiness is part of the journey, not a goal for those who experience the most superficially. Quality of experience is more rewarding than quantity of experience. As truth is revealed and reconciled, Sevens may experience positive traits of the One: balance and strength in the body, wisdom, and integrity of self. Letting go of the gluttony of experience, Sevens are propelled back to the Seven point, plus automatically move to the Heart Point, Path of Integration at the Five. They experience a slowing of activity, a quieter mind, and getting the most from experiences at deeper levels. They observe themselves and others more, realizing a cornucopia of depth and happiness.

Levels of Evolution:

Unevolved Sevens, when being denied what they want, can be abusive and aggressive. They never know when to stop; their gluttony is never sated. They are impulsive and erratic—escape artists. Unevolved Sevens will do whatever it takes to keep them from feeling their innermost feelings. This includes drug and alcohol addictions, which numb them. They go out of control, and then may realize that they have created their worst fear: they are unhappy and unhealthy.

Average evolved Sevens maintain a steady but frantic pace of activity to feed their gluttony. They love to do things and often develop a connoisseur approach. Like Fours, they can be very picky and worldly, knowing the proper manners. They cannot say no to themselves, and at times may seem out of control with activities. Kelly, a Seven, was so active and planned so much that she would not stop. She planned five to seven events every weekend. Eventually, she stopped activity when her body froze up and she ended up in the hospital, where she had to relax. Sevens are materialistic, always seeking more. They can be demanding and narcissistic.

Evolved Sevens find happiness is inside themselves and not in the materialism they experience at lower levels. With this knowing, they achieve their basic need to be happy. Evolved Sevens let go of their incessant activity and narcissism; they are enthusiastic and extroverted. They begin to experience life in depth and realize the goodness in the universe.

13 Enneatype Eight: The Boss

AKA: Confronter, Challenger, Loner, Bully
Caricatures: Tony Soprano (from the TV show, "The Sopranos") Rick Blaine (from the movie, "Casablanca") Sonny Corleone (from the movie, "The Godfather")
Fixation / Passion: Lust / Vengeance
Speech Pattern: Commands
Basic Need: Arrogance, vengeance, self-protection
Worst Fear: Being controlled and hurt by others; having their boundaries violated
Mottos: "Only the strong survive."
          "My way or the highway!"
          "I am the great and powerful Oz!"
Spirituality – Lost or Given Away: Innocence
Projected Mirror: Revenge

Growing Up:

As children, Eights learned to protect themselves from harmful environments. Many Eight children grew up with violence, and felt they constantly had to be alert to protect themselves against parents, friends, siblings, and strangers. They learned to react before they could think. Thinking delayed the time it took to protect themselves; therefore, Eights do before they think. They learned to repress feelings, believing that

feelings were for the weak: "Only the strong survive."
They saw predators consume prey, and the strong
(patriarchs and matriarchs) dominate the weak
(fathers or mothers). They learned that "people who
control win." Because they were not allowed to grow
up in the innocence and strength of Essence, Eight
children developed the strength and energy for excess
action and lust.

Eight children dominated other children and
tried to seize control—they were the bullies. They
made up the rules, expected everyone else to obey,
and broke the rules themselves to show how powerful
they were.

General Traits:

Eights are Body-based, Instinctual types. Their
feelings are repressed, while their doing is dominant
and supported by thinking. Dominance and action
allow Eights to expand their energies outward onto
the world, creating boundaries that are expansive.
This strategy gives Eights the opportunity to protect
themselves from a distance; they are not concerned
with others unless others invade their expansive
territories. Doing before thinking creates impulsive
tendencies. Eights are very impulsive, and go after
what they want in a lustful manner.

Expanding their energy boundaries onto the
world gives Eights the illusion of being powerful
people. Their energies can be felt as they walk into a
room. They command being noticed by others, and
are very aggressive and assertive. Their lust for life is
so great that they seem to be imbued with all the

energies of the universe. They are the last ones left standing at parties, trying to get other people to stand up with them to keep drinking (or drugging) and debating. Eights love debates and confrontations. They will stay awake into the middle of the night making their points. Their expansive energies and lustful lifestyles make Eights too loud, too big, and too much for many people to tolerate.

Eights have little respect for people who do not stand up to them; they see it as weakness. Eights prefer other people to be up front and to the point. They do not have time to listen to the whole story. Give them the summary or bottom line first, and provide the details only if they ask for them. Eights are blunt, and expect those around them to be the same. They talk with introjections and commands: "Do this!" "Do that!" "Because I said so!" and find it difficult to understand another person's point of view.

Eights are the most controlling of the Enneatypes, and try to control possessions, territory, and people. They sometimes feel that people around them are possessions, and thus are very protective of their significant relationships. They are supportive of underdogs, looking for justice, truth, and fairness, and can be pretty good defense attorneys.

Like Threes, Eights are very productive and accomplish a great deal, especially in the business world. Unlike Threes, Eights do not care about how they look doing it, or what people think of them. They can be like "the bull in the China shop" or the "benevolent dictator."

Eights love to make the rules, and expect other people to abide by their rules. This is especially true

in the business world: "My way or the highway!"
Eights will break their own rules because they can,
and usually other people do not say anything nor
challenge them. How do you stop a bully? Get right
up in his face and challenge him. Unfortunately,
Eights' passion is vengeance. Though they may back
down initially, they will regroup and go back at those
who challenge them. Rules to Eights are restrictive,
and many Eights feel they do not have to follow rules.
They often test the limits and consequences of
breaking rules.

Eights have excessive ways of doing and
thinking. They have "all or nothing" attitudes; either
it is right or wrong, good or bad, warrior or wimp, fair
or unfair. Though they could be multi-taskers, Eights
concentrate on one thing at a time, giving it all of
their energy. They may switch opinions on a whim.

Eights use denial as a defense mechanism.
They do not know when to stop, and think they are
stronger than they really are. They do not understand
limitations or recognize their own, thinking they have
none. Eights often are loners because people are
afraid to be around them and their explosive natures.
When they have friends, they are appreciative of
them and try to protect them.

Professionally, Eights make good leaders and
managers, and excel in areas where major changes
need to be made.

Wing Subtypes:

As the movement of energy flows through the
Enneagram, we are not limited to one type of

behavior that puts us into predefined boxes. As ego increases its control over us, we tend to fixate at a specific type or aspect of the Enneagram. As ego relinquishes control and the self-actualized personality emerges, energy flows move us constantly as we develop strategies for life based on higher states of the Enneagram. These may be known as holy ideas, virtuous flow, and etcetera.

The energy flows allow us to move to one of the adjacent Enneatypes, which are called the Wing subtypes. Although it is more common for most people to live on one of the Wing subtypes, we have found that the more self-actualized a person is, the fewer behavioral patterns develop at one subtype. Many of the people we know exhibit behavior that is balanced between the two subtypes of the main Enneatype.

The Eight at the Seven – Sevens are Head-based Thinking types; Eights are Body-based Instinctual types. Sevens are known for their multi-tasking and ability to be playful. Eights are strong and powerful. Sevens fixate on gluttony, Eights on lust (lustful gluttons?). Sevens need happiness from experiencing many things; Eights need truth and trust. Both types are materialistic. Eights at Seven are very charismatic like Sevens, and know how to get support for their ideas using charm and flattery. Eights at Seven are the most independent of subtypes. They are outgoing and love to take risks, thinking that they are powerful and unstoppable. They do not recognize their limitations. They love fights and will not back down until they win, sometimes by exhausting their opponents. The combination of Seven's impulsive nature and Eight's impulsive nature creates a very impulsive person as the Eight moves to Seven. This subtype includes Barbara Walters and Bette Davis.

The Eight at the Nine – Both Nines and Eights are Body-based instinctual types. Nines are known for their passivity, ability to see both sides of the story, and mediation skills. Eights are expansive, and see only their side of the story. Nines fixate on sloth, Eights on lust. Nines need peace and harmony; Eights like to rile things up. Since both Eight and Nine are Body-based types, Eights at Nine are well grounded. Like withdrawn, docile Nines, Eights at Nine are not as aggressive as Eights or the other subtype. Nines are plodders who cannot be forced to do anything, and this is true of the Eight at Nine as well. They are family-oriented people who control and protect their homes. Like Nines, they are stubborn and introspective. They love for others to underestimate them because these misperceptions allow Eights at Nine to control people. Nines have quiet tempers, exploding infrequently and getting through it quickly. Eights at Nine have similar types of tempers. This subtype includes Sean Connery and Indira Gandhi.

Path of Integration (Heart Points):

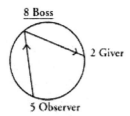

Eights move to Two when relaxed. They cease thinking about themselves so much and become more giving and philanthropic. They value friendships and are less controlling of them. At the Heart Point, Eights listen to and understand other people because—to truly grow—they must open up their feelings. At Two, they do. They move forward at Two, supporting other people.

Path of Disintegration (Stress Points):

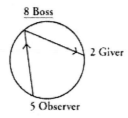

When experiencing undue stress, Eights move to Five. Realizing that their striving for control and power (and dealing with people by bullying them) is not working, Eights move to the Stress Point of Five. They withdraw into themselves to lick their wounds and regroup, looking for ways to get back at those who challenge their strength. They brood and remain secretive. Deteriorating further, they can become irritated and caustic, attacking rivals for vengeance and pushing significant others away from them. They realize their worst fear: losing strength and control.

Eights who allow the real cause of the hurt to arise may find that the best control is no control, and that being themselves does not mean overdoing security to the point of projecting expansive energy. They realize that they react before thinking because they learned in childhood to react to a hostile environment by attacking first. As truth is revealed and reconciled, Eights may experience positive traits of the Five: they focus on their inner world and relax their minds; they become compassionate. In letting go of the lust, Eights are propelled back to the Eight point, plus automatically move to the Heart Point, Path of Integration at the Two. They experience openness of feeling, deep caring and concern for others, and tenderness for themselves and others.

Levels of Evolution:

Unevolved Eights can be dictatorial and ruthless. They use their energy, vengeance, and power to push people out of the way to get what they think they need: safety and security. Ironically, this type of behavior creates revolutionary traits in people who are pushed, and gives unevolved Eights what they fear most: being harmed by others. They can be reckless and brutal, destroying everything in their path. At the extreme, they are sociopathic and may commit murder.

Average evolved Eights cherish independence and do not like to depend on other people for help, refusing to acknowledge that they may need help. To be independent, Eights realize they need to work hard and save money. They take calculated risks and may be quite conservative when investing because they hate to lose anything and are very possessive. They are expansive and controlling of those around them, and try to get obedience through threats and manipulation. Average Eights are egocentric and self-serving, but give the impression that they are protecting others and themselves. Average Eights are arrogant and believe that their powers are great. They love confrontations and will not back down from them.

Evolved Eights reawaken their feelings and find that the best control is no control. They stop trying to manipulate and control other people, and find security in balancing their lives away from excesses. They develop virtuous traits such as courage, true giving, compassion, surrender, and empathy. Evolved Eights know their limitations and stay within them. They are very resourceful and have strong inner drives towards worthwhile endeavors. They can be strong natural leaders.

14 Type Nine: The Mediator

AKA: Peacemaker, Optimist, Comforter
Caricatures: Frankie Paige (from the movie, "Stigmata") Bob Cratchit (from the book and movie, "A Christmas Carol")
Fixation / Passion: Sloth / Sloth
Speech Pattern: Sagas
Basic Need: Indecision, peace, and harmony
Worst Fear: Lost and separated from themselves; violence and disharmony
Mottos: "Easy does it."
     "Peace at any price."
     "I don't really care—let's do it your way."
Spirituality – Lost or Given Away: Significance
Projected Mirrors: Inferiority

Growing Up:

As children, Nines realized it was easier to go along with others than to confront them. They learned to diminish themselves to keep peace and harmony in their families, and fell asleep (indolence) to the love and warmth of their essential selves. Minimizing their real identity to maintain peace creates sloth: the unwillingness to choose a direction, to act, or to move with assertiveness.

Nines learned to repress anger and their own will because their needs were not met as children.

They felt they lacked the courage to ask for what they needed, so they turned off their desires. To maintain any sense of self, they learned to be passive-aggressive and stubborn. Nines often became the peacemakers at home, and helped settle family conflicts. Their worst fear is separation and annihilation: not being part of anything or anyone. They learned to refer to themselves as "nobody special," and felt they were not important enough to receive love.

General Traits:

Nines are withdrawn types. Their doing functions are repressed, so they spend a lot of time within feeling. Nines are easygoing people who strive for peace and harmony in both their internal and external environments. Their desire for harmony is so great that Nines may go to the extreme of emotional straight-lining (anhedonia – emotional flat line) to keep peace. At that point they become like zombies; they space out and detach from real life and their needs. Straight-lining emotions keep them from living life to its fullest.

Nines hate conflict and anger—not only their own anger that disturbs their inner peace, but also the anger of others that disturbs external peace. They will avoid it to the extent that they will say, "I do not care. Let's do it your way." Nines like to look for other people with whom to merge their lives. They need someone who will give them direction and support. Merging allows Nines to feel alive. They numb themselves so much that they need to merge to feel external love and warmth.

Nines are easygoing, affable, friendly, and approachable. They are open-minded and see all sides of the story. This trait gives them great skill in mediating and helping others through problems. Unfortunately, in their own lives Nines see everything as being equal. With no priorities, they have a difficult time making decisions and helping themselves. At times they may seem overwhelmed by the things they have to do, and may choose to do nothing and numb themselves further. They may turn into couch potatoes, becoming addicted to television, reading, or anything else that will keep them emotionally even. This coping strategy is replacing essential needs with unessential needs.

Indecision makes Nines into procrastinators. They do not know what to do and look externally for help, usually in the form of friends and significant others. Nines cannot say no; they will agree to do things even though they really do not want to, all for the preservation of peace and harmony. This strategy develops into internal rage, as their needs are not met. On the surface, their needs seem similar to those of the people with whom they associate. When pushed, Nines withdraw and become stubborn; they like to do things within their own timeframes. They may appear to be doing, so (unlike with Enneatype Five and Four), it is difficult to tell when they withdraw. They can be passive-aggressive and stubborn.

The defense mechanism used by Nines is narcotization. They withdraw into their inner sanctums and fantasize about peace and harmony with obsessive thoughts. Fantasizing further numbs them to the real world, which frustrates those around them.

Nines make good therapists, mediators, ministers, and referees. They excel in areas in which they feel they are needed.

Wing Subtypes:

As the movement of energy flows through the Enneagram, we are not limited to one type of behavior that puts us into predefined boxes. As ego increases its control over us, we tend to fixate at a specific type or aspect of the Enneagram. As ego relinquishes control and the self-actualized personality emerges, energy flows move us constantly as we develop strategies for life based on higher states of the Enneagram. These may be known as holy ideas, virtuous flow, and etcetera.

The energy flows allow us to move to one of the adjacent Enneatypes, which are called the Wing subtypes. Although it is more common for most people to live on one of the Wing subtypes, we have found that the more self-actualized a person is, the fewer behavioral patterns develop at one subtype. Many of the people we know exhibit behavior that is balanced between the two subtypes of the main Enneatype.

The Nine at the Eight – Both Eights and Nines are Body-based Instinctual types. Eights are assertive and strong; Nines are passive and

withdrawn. Eights fixate on lust, Nines on sloth.
Eights need truth and trust; Nines need peace and
harmony. Nines at Eight are strong like Eights and
malleable like Nines. They can mediate the problems
of others with grace like Nines, and push their point's
home like Eights. Like Eights, Nines at Eight can be
blunt and offensive. They like to maintain
comfortable routines, ensuring peace around them.
They are more sociable than basic Nines and not as
forceful as basic Eights. This subtype includes
Whoopi Goldberg and Ronald Reagan.

The Nine at the One – Both Ones and Nines
are Body-based Instinctual types. Ones are rigid,
detail-oriented, and self-righteous. Nines are affable,
flexible, and docile. Ones fixate on anger, Nines on
sloth. Ones need perfection; Nines need peace and
harmony. Nines at One combine the analyzing
abilities of Ones with creativity of Nines. They are
friendly, but not as friendly as the other subtype.
However, like Ones, they have a greater, more serious
senses of purpose. Ones are orderly and organized,
and seek harmony in their external world. This
strategy fits right in with the Nines' striving for
external and internal harmony. This subtype
includes George Lucas and Abraham Lincoln.

Path of Integration (Heart Points):

Nines move to Three when relaxed. At Three, Nines' energies increase, and decisions are easier to make. They feel a sense of purpose and direction, accomplishing tasks and looking to be accepted for who they are. At Three, Nines balance themselves.

Path of Disintegration (Stress Points):

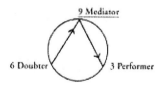

When experiencing undue stress, Nines move to Six. Realizing that staying in their inner sanctum at all costs is not productive and not working (the chaos continues no matter how much they move to straight-line emotional responses), Nines move to the

Stress Point at Six. Here they experience scattered and frantic activity. There is no time to get everything done and everyone seems to be demanding something from them. They search for meaning in relationships or belief systems. Deteriorating, they feel unhappiness and the chaos continues. Passive-aggressive tendencies die, and rage may surface as they blame others for the increased stress. At Six, they can be paranoid and extremely doubting. They may lose any sense of who they are and the reality that remained. Here they will experience their worst fear: annihilation.

Nines may stop and notice the feelings of anger that exploded from sloth, feelings that contains a truth that needs to be seen and reconciled. They may recognize that their lives and opinions do count, that they are good enough and have many qualities that are constructive and meaningful, and that they can be seen and heard rather than resort to the slothfulness they developed in childhood. As the truth is revealed and reconciled, Nines may experience positive traits of the Six: they become outgoing and friendly, secure with themselves, and serene. In letting go of sloth, Nines are propelled back to the Nine Point, plus automatically move to the Heart Point, Path of Integration at the Three. Here they experience high energy, focus on tasks, and want to be loved for who they are rather than for the person they seemed to be when they merged with those around them. They find their ideas and feelings are authentic and meaningful.

Levels of Evolution:

Unevolved Nines want to avoid dealing with problems, so they tune out and become ineffective. They fall asleep and numb themselves to the outside world. They may become catatonic in their desire to escape from reality and conflict; amnesia and dissociation may result. At this point, they create their greatest fear: annihilation and separation from the world through not being able to function. People they associate with will move away from them, which drives Nines deeper into themselves, since they will have no one with whom to merge.

Average evolved Nines live through other people by merging with them. They cannot say no and blindly go along with others, which may cause anger to arise passively. They may vent their anger in short bursts, then recompose themselves and hold it in. They do not like changes, and will resist change stubbornly. Minimizing problems, Nines withdraw or even deny there are problems. They space out, fantasize, and become oblivious and inattentive. There is a resignation of self in Nines' constant striving to keep peace at any price.

Evolved Nines find importance within themselves. They no longer believe they are "nobody special," and find purpose and direction by connecting with Essence within themselves. There, they find true peace and harmony. Presence, compassion, trust, and empathy arise, as Nines are self-actualized.

Part III: Making Our Way Back

In every moment, there is perfection and purpose. It is not important that we see the perfection and know the purpose. What is important is that we know there is perfection and purpose in every moment.

Justin E. Tomasino Jr., Ph.D.

15 How the Enneatypes Communicate

Communication is a duality—there is a communicator and a listener. Sometimes the communicator and the listener can be the same person. For communication to be effective, the communicator and the listener must be in harmony. Each party in a communication has a responsibility: the communicator is expected to convey the message in a concise way that coincides with the level of the listener; the listener is expected to ascertain the message being conveyed. Easy, right? Maybe not! If this process were so easy, then why is there such a widespread lack of communication?

There are three basics to be considered in communicating:

1. We communicate continuously; there is no way to stop communicating. Even if we climbed a mountain and sat alone, we would communicate with nature and with ourselves.

2. How many times does someone think you said something, or put meaning into a message you communicated, but it was not the message you meant to send? This may happen frequently if

there are large cultural gaps between the speaker and the listener. It also occurs when a person associates your message with something that happened to him or her in the past, and therefore is not being present with your communication. The message received is not necessarily the message transmitted.

3. Communicating involves several levels, and the message you send includes verbal and nonverbal communications. The way you send it denotes the relationship you have with the listener.

There are two types of communication, verbal and nonverbal, and they occur simultaneously. Verbal communication is an attempt to express our thoughts and feelings through the use of words. Nonverbal communication is the way in which the message is conveyed.

In verbal communication, the words used are limited by their meanings, which can vary with the communicator, the listener, or both. A word used in a connotative sense is actually the difference in the meaning of the word to each person involved in a communication. The meaning of a word may vary with its use, and slang and jargon can confuse the matter even further. For instance, when the word "bad" is used, does it mean "not good" or "good"? It could be either, depending on how it is used and the inflection and body language of the communicator. The 1890s often were referred to as the "Gay Nineties." If this term had been used to describe the

1990s, most people would have understood it quite differently!

Another area of confusion in the English language is that the prefix "in" generally changes the meaning of the root word to its opposite. For example, "complete" and "incomplete" have opposite meanings, as do "congruent" and "incongruent." But what about "flammable" and "inflammable"? They mean the same thing! The prefix "pro" generally is positive. For example, the words "promote," "progress," and "provide" typically are used positively. But what about the word "prohibit"?

When communicating in English and many other languages, we are limited by the use of pronouns. When certain Chinese or Aramaic characters are translated into English, the translator assigns a pronoun. For example, when we communicate about a deity, we use "he," "she," "him," or "her." The other choice is "it", but not too many people use "it" to describe the Creator. The Bible's interpreters choose to use "him" or "he," which leads many people to believe that the deity is male or masculine in character. The original language did not imply a gender; gender limits the All-That-Is. In the *Tao Te Ching,* the original Chinese character denoting God (Master) has no gender, but when translated into English, a gender is assigned by the translator.

The word "sinister," when used in the Bible usually refers to a person who is evil. However, "sinister" is derived from the Latin word "siniste," which means left-handed. The meaning of the word changed during the time of the Roman Empire because the Romans were typically right-handed. In England, people drive on the left side of the road instead of the right because of the time when the Romans invaded England. Since the Romans were right-handed, they marched with their sword in their right hand and their shield in their left hand. They wanted anyone approaching them to come from the right side, or the sword side. As the Romans marched in England, they stayed on the left and tried to keep their enemies on the right, thus creating the road direction. Anyone who was left-handed could shake a Roman's hand with his right hand and stab him with the left hand—which is how sinister came to mean evil and threatening. We wonder if the word "sinister" in the Bible really means left-handed. If so, it would alter the way we view people who are "sinister." Denotative uses of words are the actual differences in the use of the word. For example, "submit" could be used to mean either giving someone something or surrendering to something. How well the listener understands what is being conveyed depends upon both the content of the communication and the nonverbal signals of the communicator.

The communicator's greatest difficulty is determining how to convey his feelings accurately with words. If words are limited by their meanings, but feelings are unlimited, how can you explain a feeling with words? If someone asks what an apple tastes like, you can simply say, "It tastes like an apple." But what if the other person has never tasted an apple? He would not know what an apple tastes like. Furthermore, not all apples taste the same. The best response is to offer him a bite of the apple, and then he will know what it tastes like. Another way to communicate feeling is through nonverbal communication.

Nonverbal communication conveys the feelings of the communicator. The way the thought is conveyed with voice inflection is nonverbal. Besides the inflection, the pitch of the voice and the speed of the delivery are considered. One must be cautious when considering these factors. For example, you may say, "You're bad." That could mean two different things, depending upon the inflection. A strain in the voice of the speaker (or listener) could mean a reluctance to express oneself or it could mean the person has a sore throat or tight jockey shorts. If someone speaks slowly, it could be a sign of depression, anxiety, fear, drug use, or a disability. It also could mean that the person is from Oklahoma. If someone speaks quickly, it could be from nervousness, mania, drugs, enthusiasm, or knowledge of the subject. It also could mean that the person is from New York City.

The communicator's posture is nonverbal, and is important for conveying the proper message. Nonverbal communication includes body language. If the person with whom you are trying to communicate folds her arms, it could signify that she doesn't want to interact. It also could mean she is cold. Avoidance of eye contact could denote a lack of confidence or avoidance. It could also mean that eye contact is not acceptable in one's culture, or that the speaker considers the listener an authority figure. When someone sitting at a table leans toward you in a conversation, that person is interested in the conversation. Conversely, if the person leans back, he is not interested; he doesn't "come to the table." If someone takes off her glasses while you are speaking, she may not see your point. If she rubs the back of her neck, she may think you are a pain in the neck.

One way a speaker knows that the listener is listening is when the listener provides feedback on what is being said. A common technique is for the listener to paraphrase back to the speaker what she thinks he said: "What I believe I hear you saying is . . ."

Another effective technique is to ask questions of the speaker to ascertain the real message. Asking questions does not necessarily mean that the listener is listening, however; the motivation for asking questions may be to divert the speaker from the subject. When a person is receiving a reprimand, she may ask questions in an attempt to minimize the importance of the matter.

In our counseling work, we use an effective technique when dealing with couples that are not communicating. When couples come to us, we assume the first step is to get them to communicate properly. We give them a subject—any subject will do, including obscure subjects like raising honeybees. We ask one of them to begin by stating a sentence. The other person must state the second sentence. The first person states the third sentence, and so on. It is interesting to hear what is being said, and the couple finds that they must listen to one another to in order to formulate the next sentence. Eventually a vivid dialogue occurs. Sometimes, rather than sentences, we ask each person to state just one word of a sentence. They alternate back and forth; constructing sentences and stories one word at a time.

Effective communication must be present for people to understand each other. The nine Enneatypes each have different ways of communicating; one way to recognize a type is by the speech pattern. A friend of ours could not figure out what type he was, and labored over it. Finally he asked us our opinion. After listening to his choices and his debate over those choices, we told him we thought he was a Nine. He asked why, and we explained that there were two reasons: He could not decide on the type himself, which is a good indication of an Enneatype Nine, and he was demonstrating this with his speech pattern of long sagas and stories. After careful consideration, he agreed with our assessment and declared himself a Nine—the first step in transformation.

Following is a brief synopsis of the communication methods employed by each Enneatype.

Speech Patterns and Demeanors

Type	Speech Pattern	Hornevian Group	Demeanor
One	Preach and Teach	Assertive	Rigid and Proper
Two	Flattery, Seduction, Histrionics	Compliant	Animated and Fluid
Three	Self-Promotion	Assertive	Reserved and Athletic
Four	Melodramatic, Melancholy dialogue	Withdrawn	Loose, Animated, and Fluid
Five	Erudite, Knowledgeable	Withdrawn	Rigid and Tense
Six	Teams, "isms"	Compliant	Tense and Athletic
Seven	Quips	Compliant	Fluid and Animated
Eight	Commands	Assertive	Intrusive and Animated
Nine	Sagas	Withdrawn	Fluid and Comfortable

One: Ones, as Perfectionists, think they know what is right and what is wrong. They did the research and thought about it for a long time before they risked being incorrect and made a determination of right and wrong. Because they did all the work, they need to tell you about their findings. They view certain behavior and characteristics as perfect, and will let you know through preaching what you should do to attain perfection. For instance, they may say, "Follow the words of Jesus. Jesus will save you. Here are the words of Jesus."

Ones will research options, tell you what the best option is, and instruct you through teaching. "When looking for a new car, there are three cars to consider. I did the research, and the Toyota Camry should be your choice." "I brought this red wine to dinner because it goes best with pasta." Their voices are usually reserved and tight. They speak moderately and precisely, and do not often speak with emotion.

When Ones move to the Stress Point of Four, they withdraw and become more introspective. Their speech patterns focus on themselves and how bad they feel; they may burst out with emotion. When Ones move to the Heart Point of Seven, they are more animated, talk quickly, and smile more.

Ones are fastidious and present themselves as well groomed, well dressed, and proper. They are rigid in body stance and project energy forward, as do the other Assertive types.

Two: Twos, being Givers, need other people to need them, and they crave attention. In order to achieve these goals, Twos learned speech patterns designed to attract people. They use flattery, telling others things that make them feel good: "You look good tonight." "You are the smartest person I have ever met." Twos seduce others with their speech. Seduction opens up other people and provides opportunities for Twos to be needed ("I will help you do that"). Seductive speech does not necessarily imply sexuality, though it often does: "If you changed your hairstyle, you would have to beat men off with a stick."

Twos attract other people by being consoling—they are the first ones to approach people in need. They will put their arms around a person and give warm hugs when needed. Twos speak with emotion and often rattle on, utilizing histrionics, dramatization, hysterics, and etcetera. They may speak rapidly.

When Twos move to the Stress Point of Eight, they become louder and more demanding in their speech patterns. They can be quite animated and abusive, telling people how ungrateful they are for not needing them. When Twos move to the Heart Point of Four, they slow down and become more introspective, speaking more about themselves.

Twos, wanting to attract other people, are well groomed, well dressed, and presentable. They often will dress and act seductively, which does attract other people. They project energy outwardly for the purpose of helping others, and exude warmth and friendliness. Twos are very fluid and animated in their bodies.

Three: Threes, as performers, want to be recognized through their achievements. They speak in patterns that let others know their profession and how good they are at getting things done. Their speech pattern is that of self-promotion: "I am the best real estate agent in town. I am efficient and sell houses faster than anyone else."

Threes are good networkers and enjoy talking with people. They will charm others and ask questions to find out the person's profession and talents, looking for opportunities to use them to further their career. They will deceive others, leading them to believe they are really interested in them. They talk rapidly and efficiently. Threes usually do not speak with emotion, but if they sense emotion is needed, they will use it. When we stop and think about what the Three said, we realize that the Three said what we wanted to hear, but there was little or no substance and much puffing.

When Threes move to the Stress Point of Nine, they slow down and become introspective. Their speech patterns get scattered as they lose control of their feelings. When Threes move to the Heart Point of Six, they speak more of teamwork.

Threes, who need to let people know how good they are, usually are impeccably groomed and well dressed, and know how to dress appropriately for different occasions. They project energy outwardly while maintaining control, especially of emotions. Threes are warm and friendly when they feel it is necessary in order to be the most efficient. Threes are reserved in their bodies and can be very athletic and competitive.

Four: Fours, romantics who focus on what is missing and look for saviors, need to have other people see them as significant and different. Fours detest commonality and the mundane, and their speech patterns convey their search for significance. They tend to focus on emotions, forming melodramatic, melancholic dialogue. They need to let everyone know they are different. They are moody, and often move from manic speech patterns to depressive speech patterns in one conversation: "I am so different, nobody recognizes who I am. Why do other people not notice me? Aren't I good enough? Nobody ever notices me." They speak of sadness and abandonment, trying to elicit pity from those around them. Fours may speak rapidly or slowly, and always with emotion.

When Fours move to the Stress Point of Two, they move outwardly and try to impress other people to avoid loneliness. They may try too hard to get others to like them. They can be seductive and flattering. When Fours move to the Heart Point of One, they become more serious and disciplined with their speech patterns. They become more real and fantasize less.

Fours, needing to feel special, dress, groom, and behave uniquely. They may be flamboyant and move their arms and bodies to convey it. They usually do not project energy outwardly and remain withdrawn; however, they can be quite crass and demeaning if they think others have scorned them. Fours are loose in their bodies, and can be quite fluid and dramatic in movement.

Five: Fives, who observe, need to think they have enough knowledge to get by in life. When they communicate with others, it is in the style of showing how smart and competent they are. The speech pattern used is to convey that they are erudite and knowledgeable. Speaking with Fives can be like reading a thesis or dissertation. They often quote experts and authors to show that they know what they are talking about: "Gerry Spence, in his book said . . ." "Deepak Chopra in a speech in Seattle said . . ." "Einstein's theory of relativity states . . ." Quoting others does not necessarily mean that Fives agree with the authors. When confronted and asked for their own opinions, Fives may ask questions to divert attention from themselves. They also may continue quoting others without directly answering the questions.

Fives control conversations by asking questions, seemingly to accumulate knowledge. They may speak rapidly (especially if they are busy trying to finish a project), and rarely speak with emotion. They usually don't raise their voices unless they have gone to the Heart Point of Eight, at which they will be more assertive. Fives prefer to communicate through e-mail, postcards, mail, and telephone because they shun one-on-one, direct contact.

When Fives move to the Stress Point of Seven, they can be short, sarcastic, and scattered in their speech. When they move to the Heart Point of Eight, they speak more assertively, talk more about feelings, can be loud, and may even express anger.

Fives are loners and prefer to dress casually. The males may have beards and long hair, and often are "geeky" types. Their energy is withdrawn. When talking with a Five, you may have to keep moving forward as they are moving backward, but do not push them into a corner. Five are usually rigid and tense in their bodies.

Six: Sixes, as fearful, anxious types, look for security and safety in groups, teams, organizations, and belief systems. Speech patterns identify which team or "ism" they are expounding: "We can get through this together as a team." "Buddhism brings peace and serenity into my life." Sixes scan the environment, searching for danger, and are alert and ready for worst-case scenarios: "If I get fired—and I think I will—I will have to update my resume, and I know where I can go for a new job." They may speak rapidly, especially in panic situations. Sixes tend to be accusatory and blame others for what goes wrong. They can be cynical and probing, asking questions to validate their inner suspiciousness.

When they move to the Stress Point of Three, they can be quite manic in their speech, usually when discussing fearful situations. When they move to the Heart Point of Nine, Sixes' speech slows down as they ease their minds and their fearful outlooks.

Sixes are Compliant types. They need to fit in to wherever they belong, so they will groom and dress appropriately. Their energy is usually projected outwardly as they scan the environment for safety; however, they tend to withdraw at times. Counter-phobic Sixes lean toward you when speaking, and phobic sixes lean back. Sixes generally are tense in their bodies.

Seven: Sevens consider themselves epicures and dilettantes; they seek happiness by planning and experiencing a multitude of things. They speak in quip styles in an effort to get attention and keep those around them laughing (at times, they may sound like Groucho Marx). Sevens use charm to attract others, and they love to have a variety of people around them.

Sevens can be seductive like Twos, but will not commit like Twos—Sevens need variety. They want other people to enjoy being around them. Their speech patterns tend to include a sense of entitlement to enjoy life, and they talk constantly about their plans: "I will go to the movies, and then to the party across town. If that party is a bummer, I'll go to the museum and walk around until the other party starts later." "You do your thing, I will do mine." Sevens are usually loud, but not as loud as Eights.

When Sevens move to the Stress Point of One, they become more serious and critical in their speech patterns. When they move to the Heart Point of Five, they speak less and are more introspective, talking more about feeling bad.

Sevens like to be the center of attention at parties, and groom and dress well for the occasion. They can be quite animated and forward; however, their compliant natures will make them fit in rather than be mavericks. Sevens are fluid in motion. They are great people to be around if you like a lot of activity, but not so great if you want to talk about internal feelings and emotions.

Eight: Eights feel secure by dominating and controlling others. Their speech patterns are filled

with commands and introjections: "Do it my way!"
"My way or the highway!" "Sit down and listen!"
Eights have problems listening to other people; they
are narcissistic and concentrate on themselves and
their needs. Eights are loud and boisterous. Their
voices carry a long way, and can be booming.

When Eights move to the Stress Point of Five,
they become more introspective and withdrawn. They
feel sorry for themselves and let others know about it.
When they move to the Heart Point of Two, Eights
talk more of helping others. They can be seductive
and flattering.

Eights do not care what other people think
about them. They dress and groom the way they want
to, and can go from sweat suits to tuxedos. Their
energies expand outwardly, as do the other Assertive
types. Eights can fill the room in their effort to be the
center of attention. They are animated, lean into
people, and move intrusively, shaking hands and
patting others on the back.

Nine: Nines, mediators who see both sides of
the story, want other people to notice and respect
them. They want to feel worthwhile. In an effort to
achieve this, when they get their turn to speak, they
speak in sagas—long stories that provide every little
detail. People who prefer summaries (such as Threes
and Eights) have difficulty listening to Nines. Nines
seek peace and harmony. Through their speech
patterns, they focus on what they do or will do to
provide harmony in their lives. They can be loud at
times, but usually they speak in more reserved tones,
perhaps even a monotone.

When Nines move to the Stress Point of Six, they may chatter about how everything is falling apart. When they move to the Heart Point of Three, they become more efficient, rapid, and precise in their speech.

Nines are Withdrawn types; they can dress and groom to fit in with others—or not. They can be mavericks like Fours. Nines' energy stays within, but it is less noticeable than with Fours and Fives because Nines are more comfortable in their bodies. They can be quite fluid and animated if they need to be.

16 True Intimacy: What It's All About

Intimacy requires emotional involvement with ourselves and with other people. It involves loving, closeness, and caring. Intimacy requires commitment of self and depth of character—a depth of character that can be achieved only with vertical integration. It means being ourselves in love, without judgment, comparison, or the need to be right. In the duality of right and wrong, if we believe we are right, then someone else must be wrong

Intimacy requires nourishment of self and others. As plants and trees need fresh air, water, food, and light to grow, intimacy needs space, time, and light to flourish. If we pull up plants to examine the roots, we will kill the plants. If we dissect intimate relationships and examine them too closely, they will die.

When we look at a rose, we see there is a beautiful flower, but under the flower are thorns. We are much the same: there are thorns beneath our flowers. We know the rose by the flower, not by the thorns. If we look closely at a diamond, we see that the diamond has flaws. As the rose has its thorns and the diamond has its flaws, we have our flaws. It is our flaws that make us unique and allow us to manifest the special gifts we were born with. Do the thorns on the roses make the roses less beautiful?

Do the flaws on the diamond make the diamond less beautiful? Why do we think that our flaws make us less beautiful? How many of us live each day punishing ourselves because of our thorns and flaws and totally miss the flowers?

Intimacy requires unconditional acceptance of others and ourselves. It means being tolerant, kind, gentle, and respectful of self and others. If we do not accept and love ourselves unconditionally, and cannot be kind, tolerant, and respectful toward ourselves—if we do not care for ourselves, we cannot feel these things for other people.

Most of us have difficulty being intimate. Intimacy allows others to see our real selves, as well as allowing our real selves to project outward on to other people. If we do not let others in, we cannot be intimate. If we cannot let ourselves out, we cannot be intimate. How many people say they give and give, letting themselves out, but receive nothing in return? When they are looking for something in return, they have not truly given. They let themselves out conditionally, with the expectation that they will satisfy their needs—which implies that they are not fully capable of meeting their own needs.

Many people complain that they let others in and constantly are abused by them. But are they really letting people in? In truth, they are demonstrating a lack of self-esteem. If we lie down on railroad tracks and a train runs us over, it's our own fault—we chose to lie down on the tracks. How much respect do we have for ourselves when we do these things? If we continually get involved in abusive situations, we have deluded ourselves into thinking that our needs can be met externally. We project neediness onto the environment, and guess what we get in return? The Universe gives us back what we project. Out of compassion, it replenishes what we gave away, and sends us more.

It takes whole people to be intimate. How can unbalanced people be totally open, honest, and intimate with others when they are not open, honest, and intimate with themselves? How can we let ourselves out, when we do not know the truth within? How can we let others in when we are afraid of what they may find, which will trigger our anxieties of abandonment, shame, guilt, and insecurity? How can we build walls around ourselves and claim that we are open? How can we put ourselves in boxes, hide in the depths of the deepest oceans, and say, "If you love me, you will find me?"

When ego is out of balance and dominates us, it creates fears of not being good enough—fears that if we expose our true selves, others will see us as flawed and abandon us. Why would others abandon us if they are caring, open, loving, and honest? Ego makes us think that if we were intimate with them, others will control us. This is not true intimacy. It is a trick of the ego, which lies to us, making us think we are not good enough and are too flawed to show who we truly are. Paradoxically, we fear that the Creator—who creates perfection in every moment—made a mistake in creating us.

Intimacy implies connectedness, harmony, and oneness. Ego by its very nature keeps us in the illusion of separation. Intimacy does not exist in the presence of ego.

When Enneatypes are ego imbalanced, they manifest dysfunctional behaviors out of fears that reflect upon their inability to achieve intimacy. Ego fixations prevent us from being open and allowing others to come in; we fear that they may find out who we really are and reject us. We may think that in order to prevent rejection, we must be in control of the situation so we can allow others to see only what we want them to see. We may feel we have to control others' feelings and thoughts so we can mold them into our relative views of false intimacy. We project images of what we think others will accept, even if those images are for pity (like those of Enneatype Four). We use vast amounts of energy to hide our true selves.

The Enneatypes and Intimacy

One: The Perfectionist – Relationships for Ones must be perfect. They visualize ideal relationships and try to mold themselves and others into this perfect picture. Perfection is relative in this sense, and achieving relative perfection is impossible for humans. Ones are highly structured and organized. They believe they have to be right because they already did the research and know what is perfect. Therefore, in order to manifest intimacy, there is a process of rightness. Being right means there also is a "wrong." Being wrong means we are not accepted for who we truly are.

Ones have severe inner critics that are relentless in their pursuit of perfection. They do not live up to their own models of perfection and tend to project the blame outwardly, making others believe that the relationship would be perfect if only they would change in the way the One thinks they should change. Ones equate criticism with caring and love. In arguments, they are rigid and have long memories. They are insecure and angry with themselves, projecting these insecurities to others and bringing up past mistakes and failures. Intimate relationships cannot flourish if the past is always brought forward. Ones try to control their environment by pushing outwardly and criticizing others in an attempt to get them to comply with their views of perfection.

At the Stress Point of Four, Ones begin to fantasize and daydream (as do Fours) about how intimacy should feel. They focus on what is missing in their lives, and resentment and envy fester inside them. They believe that no one appreciates them. Anger and rage rise to the surface and they explode, blaming others for their unhappiness. Reflecting on their loss of composure, Ones withdraw more into themselves and attempt to shut out the world. Understanding the source of their anger and resentment, Ones must realize that right and wrong are dualities and relative to the observer. Transcending dualities is a route to freedom. Ones need to loosen up and allow their real feelings to arise and reveal the truth within them. They can recognize tenseness and rigidity as the body holds pain associated with truth at the cellular level. Freeing themselves of burdens contained at the Stress Point, Ones propel themselves back to the One point and then to the Heart Point of Seven.

At the Heart Point of Seven, Ones experience the absolute perfection of unconditional love. They are relaxed and their bodies loosen. They are bright and funny, using quips to communicate. They are spontaneous and find a deeper meaning to life.

Two: The Giver – Twos love to give to others with the expectation of receiving love in return. However, this is not true giving, which requires nothing in return. They think that when others need them, they will be loved. Twos have difficulty giving to themselves; they do not find love within and seek it outwardly. Unfortunately, they cannot give love if they do not love themselves first, and cannot give to others until they learn to give to themselves.

Twos crave intimacy. They need to be around other people because they feed off the energy of people needing them. When they think others do not need them, they shut down and can become very bitter and sarcastic. They alter their own feelings and personality to meet the needs of others, creating another image of themselves. This confuses them and they lose touch with their true selves: "Which one is the real me?" Twos are like Nines in that they identify themselves through other people. In relationships, they may become quite co-dependent.

Twos' major problem with intimacy is that they cannot be intimate with themselves. Pride prevents them from asking for help. Twos try to control their environment by molding themselves into what they think other people need. They may become extremely critical of others, thinking they are ungrateful.

At the Stress Point of Eight, Twos become very aggressive. In an effort to get attention, they can be intrusive and meddling. They project outwardly that the reason for their unhappiness is due to being unappreciated. Like Eights, they may plan vengeance for those who scorn them. Twos at this point need help, but like Eights, they refuse outside help, preferring to punish themselves. They need to learn to help themselves before they can grow. Realizing their own needs and allowing truth to arise and be reconciled, they will propel back to the Two point and then to the Heart Point of Four.

At the Heart Point of Four, Twos withdraw and reflect on meeting their own needs. They learn to give without any expectation of receiving. Twos learn to nourish themselves first, and to love themselves for who they are.

Three: The Performer – Threes are Type A workaholics who have little quiet time for intimacy; they are too busy with their careers for true intimacy. They create false images of themselves in order to win the approval of others for their accomplishments, thus they do not know who they really are. Threes project onto others what they think others would like. They may seem caring and compassionate if that is what they think the crowd needs. Threes, like Twos, have problems identifying with their real selves. Twos alter their identities to get other people to need them; Threes alter their identities to further their accomplishments. They confuse themselves into thinking their false selves are their real selves.

Threes avoid feeling and are not romantic. Like Fives, they believe they can settle everything with logic. Threes spend most of their time working and avoid having quiet, reflective time to learn about their feelings. They like the energy rush that occurs when they initially meet people, and therefore crave dating. They love to date partners who enhance their image or those who match their projected self-image. With dating, Threes can alter their image to fit in with the crowd as they change their partners. There is an increase in energy and attention that goes along with first meeting people; this is what Threes like. Also, if Threes enjoy only the beginning energy of relationships and dating, they miss the depth of intimacy—but this is okay for fixated Threes who do not know who they really are and are terrified for others to find out.

Threes try to control their environment by altering themselves and increasing their activities, hoping to accomplish more. Doing becomes vital to maintain the Three's sense of worth.

At the Stress Point of Nine, Threes realize that their self-worth is tied to their accomplishments. Trying to accomplish more, they spend less time in meaningful, intimate relationships. Anger arises when they recognize the shallowness associated with false identity and realize that true happiness is not connected to achievements. Truth arises, and Threes may find their real selves as they feel the pain of not being valued for who they are. They reconnect with themselves and open their feelings, which propels them back to the Three point and then to the Heart Point of Six.

At the Heart Point of Six, Threes become less concerned about themselves and learn to bond more with their intimates, giving and working together for purpose. Slowing down at the Heart Point allows Threes to experience their feelings and become more expressive of who they are. They find authenticity, and deceit falls away. Knowing themselves helps them to know others. Getting close to their feelings allows them to get close to others.

Four: The Romantic – We may think of Fours—who are Romantics—to be highly intimate. Fours, like Twos, crave intimacy, but when they have the opportunity for closeness, they push people away with their push-pull defense mechanisms. Fours do not want people to know who they really are. They think they are flawed, different, and unique in an unconnected way. When people get close, they might discover that the Four is flawed, so the Four pushes them away before they get too close.

Fours do not think they are good enough to have anyone close to them. Romantics fantasize and dream about that one special person who will ride up on a white horse, recognize the Four for who he or she is, and ride off into the sunset with them. Real life and fantasies are quite different, however. Fours tell us that they would rather sleep and dream because their dreams are more exciting than real life; real life is boring. In their fantasies, Fours create what they think intimacy feels like. They compare their relationships to those feelings, and when reality does not match their fantasies, they project their insecurities onto their intimate relationships: "You don't love me. You never loved me. If you did, I would not feel this way."

Fours look at other people and their relationships and compare them to their own, thinking that other people have it better. They focus on what is missing, which creates envy: "Why are they happy and I am not?" Fours, like Twos and Threes, have identity issues. They do not know who they really are. They are terrified of what they see, and think other people who see the same thing will abandon them. This fear results in withdrawal. Fours, like Twos and Sixes, can be co-dependent, hoping that others will seek them out as in their fantasies. Fours attempt to control their intimate relationships with emotion, and try to get others to feel guilty for not showing them the love they dreamed of.

At the Stress Point of Two, Fours realize that their withdrawn behaviors have not worked. They lash out, criticizing their intimates, emoting and dramatizing to get others to notice them and fulfill their needs. At the Two point, Fours may recognize the difference between fantasy and real life. If they observe their behavior and allow truth to surface and reconcile it, they will see the essence of who they are, which will propel them back to the Four point and then to the Heart Point of One.

At the Heart Point of One, Fours become less melodramatic and more disciplined and serious. They live within the real world and see themselves for who they really are. Fours are special, as is everyone else. They need to push themselves out of their withdrawn stances and do something about their relationships to allow closeness, intimacy, and practicality to arise. When they do, they will feel very close to their intimates.

Five: The Observer – Fives prefer to observe life rather than be observed. Intimacy requires letting ourselves out. Being observed means to be open and comfortable with ourselves, not caring what others think of us. Observing means allowing ourselves to be seen through filters, like hunters in a blind. Fives are great at letting themselves out to observe, but do not like to allow others to observe them. They think that the observer does not affect the observed, but if this is really so, then why are Fives afraid to be observed?

Fives fear that others may think they are not knowledgeable enough, and thus not good enough to be intimate. Intimacy requires openness of feeling, but Fives would rather not feel. They try to reason out everything with their intellects. Feelings are not logical and rational. Fives, who are logical like Threes, are seldom romantic. They disdain feeling and look down on those who feel, thinking that feelings make humans flawed. Intimacy is painful for Fives because it involves feelings, which they try to avoid. Rather than express their feelings, they withdraw and attempt to understand their feelings with their minds.

Fives can seem cold and distant in relationships because they require the space and privacy to try to figure out life. Fives, like Ones, are structured and organized, which results in rigidity. Intimacy needs flexibility, and open-ended relationships require boundless, expansive energy. Fives are greedy with their energy, so they prefer closed-ended, predictable relationships. They try to control the environment by withdrawing into their shells, shutting down energy and further alienating their intimates.

At the Stress Point of Seven, Fives become scattered and fill time with meaningless activities in an attempt to control their racing minds. Accelerating minds create delusional thoughts and fantasies based on irrational logic. At Seven, Fives can be quite sarcastic to their intimates and may accuse them of making them look stupid. If Fives can recognize their insecurities and allow the anger to surface, they may see the truth associated with it. Reconciling the truth, Fives propel themselves back to the Five point and then to the Heart Point of Eight.

At the Heart Point of Eight, Fives become present in their bodies and with their feelings, expressing them in the moment. They come out of their shells and meet life head on. Life energy expands since they no longer feel the need to conserve it. Being present (and knowing that the observer affects the observed) allows Fives to recognize their true needs. They become closer to and more aggressive with their intimates.

Six: The Doubter – Sixes doubt their self-worth. They are fearful of the environment and have lost the faith that everything will be okay if they just let go. When Sixes come out of their shells, they scan the environment for danger. The potential for danger is all they see, even in intimate relationships. When

Sixes see danger, they withdraw into their shells. Once in a relationship, Sixes are loyal even if the relationship is harmful. They can be co-dependent like Twos, Nines, and Fours, hoping that the relationship will change when their mates change. Intimacy requires no changes, but an acceptance of individuals just the way they are.

Sixes stay in abusive relationships because their fear of the environment tells them "the devil they know is better than the devil they don't know." This fear is familiar to them, and familiarity creates numbness to change. Sixes focus on their flaws, and the flaws in their relationships make them feel guilty about their deficiencies.

Sixes have trust issues and create fights to see if their partners are as loyal and committed to the relationship as they are: "Why should she stay with me?"

They try to control the environment by moving themselves to safety. Safety is relative, and Sixes may fear that where they put themselves is not safe and may sabotage it, further exacerbating their anxieties.

At the Stress Point of Three, Sixes become driven and hard working, keeping themselves energized and engaged in activities. Like Threes, they develop deceitful images of themselves. Activities and false images do not allow Sixes time to relax with their intimates; this behavior pushes others away. If Sixes can stop and realize the truth in their fear, they may be able to reconcile it and see that the environment is—and always has been—safe. When focusing on the environment, we see what we look for. Sixes need to recognize their compulsion to look for danger, as there is wonderment, warmth, and beauty out there. This recognition will propel them back to the Six point and then to the Heart Point of Nine.

At the Heart Point of Nine, Sixes realize that they are good enough just the way they are. Sixes in abusive relationships recognize the nature of the situation and do something about it. They cease their excessive thinking and become more present in their bodies and their expression of feeling. They find they can be warm and loyal with their intimates.

Seven: The Epicure – Sevens like to keep their options open; they like variety and want to have a variety of experiences. Intimacy requires openness, commitment, and trust. Sevens, in an effort to keep their options open, avoid intimacy, which they find to be confining and restrictive. Sevens are the Enneatype most often seen in "open marriages." Their credo is, "You do your thing; I'll do mine." Intimacy, however, requires open feelings in both others and ourselves.

Sevens try to avoid deep inner feelings, from which they escape by creating a multitude of experiences to avoid feeling. For Sevens, feelings are associated with pain. Activities help narcotize and numb feelings. When in close relationships, Sevens get anxious when their partners demand anything from them, especially openness of feeling. They do not like people clinging to them because clinging restricts their movements.

Like all the other Enneatypes, Sevens project onto others the responsibility for the failure of relationships: "It is always someone else's fault, because it cannot be mine." Sevens are narcissistic and take care of themselves in an entitled way. They try to control the environment by outwardly being assertive and pushing forward, but internally they want to be left alone to do their own thing. This posture alienates intimates, as the Seven projects a lack of caring.

At the Stress Point of One, Sevens realize that there is little depth in frantic activities. They tighten up and repress their anger like Ones. This further restricts their activities, so they become irritated and sarcastic, further pushing away intimates. If Sevens can stop and see that their overactive minds have driven away their intimates, and allow anger and frustration to arise to be reconciled, they will see that activities with depth are more meaningful. Happiness is not a goal, but part of life's journey. They will propel themselves back to the Seven point and then to the Heart Point of Five.

At the Heart Point of Five, Sevens slow down and access their inner feelings, no matter how painful they may seem. They find that the closeness in intimacy will allow them the depth that was missing in endless frantic activities.

Eight: The Boss – Eights are control freaks—they want to dominate people and have things turn out their way. They use high energy and coercion, if necessary, to get others to comply. Eights' greatest fear is to be dominated and controlled by others, which they avoid by being offensive rather than defensive: "Kill or be killed." Eights like to control not only other people, but themselves as well—especially their feelings. They do not like moody people.

Eights, like Sevens, are narcissistic and take care of themselves first. There is no problem with taking care of ourselves first, but Eights do not take care of others after taking care of themselves, except for those that are close to them. Eights, taking care of others is accomplished through power and strength, as long as the others comply with their rules. Eights believe they are so powerful and above their own rules that they often do things in excess (lust). They think they are so strong that (like Twos) they will not ask for help. Twos refuse help due to pride, Eights through false strength and denial.

Intimacy requires openness and sharing. Eights hoard and are not open. They keep people from getting too close to them through the high energy they emit, creating boundaries as far out as possible. Eights try to control the environment by projecting their energies out so far that they seem to have no boundaries, intruding upon and bullying others, which pushes away intimates.

At the Stress Point of Five, Eights withdraw and enclose themselves in shells. They brood, think of ways to get even with those who are invading their boundaries, and become caustic and irritated. If Eights allow their rage to rise to the surface, they can see the truth in it and reconcile it. They will see that the best control is no control, and that the energy they use to expand their boundaries can be used for better things. This will propel them to the Eight point and then to the Heart Point of Two.

At the Heart Point of Two, Eights learn to access their real feelings, which allow them to be more open and compassionate toward others. It diminishes their boundaries and enables them to let others in. At this point, Eights do not feel they are being dominated or controlled by others. They become truly giving, and get closer to their intimates.

Nine: The Mediator – Nines crave peace and harmony. They will sell themselves out to meet these needs, even to the point of merging with those around them. Intimacy requires openness of feeling, but feelings sometimes create ripples in peace and harmony. Such disturbances are shunned by Nines, who will seek peace and harmony at any cost— including that of losing themselves and further falling asleep.

Nines do not know who they are, thus they try to merge their lives with those around them, and identify with other people rather than with themselves. If we believe we are insignificant and that our feelings do not matter, then we seek other people we think are significant and take on their lives. Like Twos, Fours, and Sixes, Nines can be co-dependent. Merging creates anger and resentment. Nines are passive-aggressive, especially when things do not work out the way they expect them to. Merging gives Nines an opportunity to blame the people with whom they have merged.

Since Nines do not know who they are, they are confused about whom to love. Seeing all sides of an issue as equally valid, they procrastinate when making decisions and avoid going into action. They prefer to narcotize themselves and fall asleep to who they really are. Not knowing who you are creates an aversion to let yourself out, which is required for intimacy. How can we let out what we do not know? When Nines are pushed to reveal themselves and make decisions, they withdraw.

Nines have low self-esteem and avoid opening themselves to others, thinking that if others see them for who they really are, they will judge them to be insignificant and will not like them. Nines tend to think people do not like them. This belief is a projection of how Nines really feel about themselves: they do not like themselves and believe that their lives are meaningless and insignificant. Nines try to control the environment by withdrawing into their inner world, numbing themselves and appearing as if they are going through the motions unconsciously.

At the Stress Point of Six, Nines go into action. Once in action, inertia keeps them moving in scattered and frantic activities. They realize that their withdrawn behaviors have not worked and that they need to do something else. They become fearful and doubting like Sixes, further thinking they are insignificant and worthless. As anger arises, they may see the truth within it and reconcile truth for what it is. This will propel them back to the Nine point and then to the Heart Point of Three.

At the Heart Point of Three, Nines open up, recognize who they really are, and present themselves to the world. They realize that their thoughts and feelings are as valid as anyone else's. They have their own lives, and within those lives is a purity of spirit and love. Nines begin to take action and assume responsibility for those actions.

17 Forgiveness: Letting Go of Our Failures

Forgiveness is the most powerful virtue that can be practiced to advance humanity to a more highly evolved state. There is much confusion about the nature of real forgiveness—it is not what most of us think it is. The term *forgiveness*, used in the ways we have become accustomed to, results in a deluded sense of forgiveness that is righteous at best. This is not real forgiveness; it is judgmental actions or thoughts. To understand forgiveness, we need to review the nature of reality and develop an understanding of the nature of the universe.

Unity of Existence

The universe is boundless; it has no end, nor did it have a beginning. Nothing exists outside the universe. In universal terms, there is no such thing as "outside." The universe is complete and whole within itself. It needs nothing to improve it, and nothing can be taken away from it. It is the totality of all existence.

The universe may be termed the "All-That-Is": there is nothing but the All-That-Is, and everything is interconnected with everything else. It is seamless, and there are no exceptions, since nothing exists beyond the All-That-Is.

The All-That-Is or universe is pure being or Essence. We may call it God, Goddess, Essence, Spirit, Vishnu, Jehovah, the Absolute, etcetera. It does not matter what it is called; in its Essence, it cannot be changed or interfered with, just as a wave cannot interfere with or change the ocean. Since the universe is all connected and all one, it is perfect the way it is. All possibilities exist in the present moment and each moment is created anew.

The universe or Essence contains absolute truth. At human levels, absolute truth is difficult to comprehend because of the duality of nature and the limits of our five physical senses. What we observe most of the time is relative, and thus cannot be absolute. If truth changes, it cannot be truth. Relative truth includes duality and is based on a point of view. It is constantly changing. Relative truth is dependent on the ego and the perception of the ego. For example, at some point in history, it was believed that the earth was the center of the universe and the sun revolved around the earth. Scientifically, we have shown that this principle was inaccurate. "Truth" was changed.

If you point in a direction and ask someone to tell you to which direction you are pointing, he may say you are pointing to the right. From your perspective, however, you are pointing to the left. If he says you are pointing to the west, that may be true—but if you were standing exactly at the North Pole, no matter which way you pointed (except for up), it would be south. This is truth relative to the observer, and it always changes.

At a deeper human level, we may experience truth in which–regardless of the relativeness and duality in a situation—there exists an Essential nature that does not change. At this level is the recognition that dual natures are part of the same whole. We see that right is not right without a definition of "wrong." We are who we are, and may see ourselves by who we are not. We find that truth is the same regardless of whether or not we exist. In the pointing example, we may realize that no matter which way we pointed, the answer would depend on our point of view. From a universal perspective, our pointing is pointless.

If we go deeper into Essence, we find that Essence is not only matter but also "no-matter." All matter manifests from no-matter. Everything is created from what seems to be nothing. We see that what exists is not only inside of us, but also exists outside of us, and is the All-That-Is. We find that at the level of absolute truth, nothing ever changes. What was, is, and always shall be. In the pointing example, we may realize that it is not really us that point. Form is an illusion— our bodies are created from nothing, and are also illusions.

Matter

Manifestation of matter is created from the no-matter. It is all energy vibrating at different frequencies, revealing matter in the human dimension. All forms are interrelated fields of energy, which at quantum levels are seamless; they are boundless. In *The Dancing Wu Li Masters,* Gary Zukav writes, "Some biologists believe that a single plant cell carries within it the capability to reproduce the entire plant. Similarly, the philosophical implication of quantum mechanics is that all of the things in our universe (including us) that appear to exist independently are actually parts of one all-encompassing organic pattern, and that no parts of that pattern are ever really separate from it or from each other."[6]

We know the human dimension of the universe through our five senses: sight, hearing, touch, smell, and taste. All that we know at this level is limited to those senses. For example, to see something, we need light. Without light, we cannot see it. Not only do we need light, we need light at certain frequencies to see it. It must be visible light. When we hear, there must be vibrations that produce sound within the range of our hearing sense. We know there is more than visible light, and that sound exists beyond the range of our hearing. Consequently, our senses are limited. More exists than what our senses perceive. There are other senses associated with the nonphysical world, senses deep within Essence or spiritual dimensions.

Gary Zukav, in *The Seat of the Soul,* writes, "We are evolving from five-sensory humans into multi-sensory humans. Our five senses, together, form a single sensory system that is designed to perceive physical reality. The perceptions of a multi-

---

[6] Gary Zukav, *The Dancing Wu Li Masters,* 48.

sensory human extend beyond physical reality to the larger dynamic systems of which our physical reality is a part. The multi-sensory human is able to perceive, and to appreciate, the role that our physical reality plays in a larger picture of evolution, and the dynamics by which our physical reality is created and sustained. The realm is invisible to the five-sensory human." [7]

There are senses beyond the five senses of our bodies. These senses are connected and linked to the universal cosmos and assist us in knowing our origins. These senses are intuitive and essential in nature. If we limit ourselves to the five physical senses, we are deluded into thinking we are separate from everything else and are alone in the universe to make our own way. Intuitively, we know that we are not alone—the universe is alive and vibrant. It is our physical senses that limit our perceived connection to Essence.

Like the patterns in a mosaic, all of the energy patterns that create physical reality are part of the whole energy pattern of the universe. Each pattern in a mosaic may be viewed as a pattern within itself, but also is part of the larger pattern that makes up the mosaic. A wave in the ocean can be viewed as wave energy, but the wave energy was created and is part of the energy of the entire ocean. The patterns vibrate at their own frequencies and are part of the frequency vibrations of the universe. Frequency patterns within us contain both the vibrations of our human dimension and the vibrational patterns of the

---

[7] Gary Zukav, *The Seat of the Soul,* 27.

universe. Therefore, we live in two worlds simultaneously: the world of humanity and the world of spirit. At the deepest levels, both worlds are the same. There are no separations and no exceptions. We cannot exist separately from the whole.

Spiritual Consciousness

Energy vibrations form patterns that appear to us as matter. All matter is composed of energy patterns and therefore are not solid, although it appears solid to us. These patterns vibrate - the higher the frequency vibration, the more complex the pattern; conversely, the lower the frequency vibration, the simpler the pattern. Matter is formed by the condensation of the light of the universe or All-That-Is, which is the highest vibrational frequency. Light consists of photons, and since light is the All-That-Is, it is conscious. Everything in the universe is conscious, including subatomic particles. Photons not only are conscious, they are organic, which implies that everything is both conscious and organic. Something is organic if it can decide what to do with the information it receives. Photons can do this.[8]

Not only is the universe conscious and organic, it moves with direction according to fixed physical laws. These laws, which come from the All-That-Is, are the same for everything in the universe, including us. Since we are connected to the universe,

---

[8] For further reading on this concept, try Gary Zukav, *The Dancing Wu Li Masters,* 63-64.

and the physical laws of the universe are from the Source, we are directly affected by the All-That-Is. Not only do the fixed physical laws provide the directional movement of the universe, this direction is also intelligent, and since the universe is conscious and organic, it moves with direction according to fixed physical laws, and does so with warmth and love. There are no random events or coincidences. As Einstein said, "God does not play dice with the universe."

The movement of the universe is an unfoldment of consciousness. According to fixed physical laws, this unfoldment is filled with warmth and love. It is perfect—nothing needs to be added and nothing needs to be taken away. Everything is just the way it should be in each moment. There are no exceptions, including us. If one ant in the universe were out of place at any given moment, the entire structure would collapse. There is freedom implied in this statement. We are exactly where we need to be and exactly the way we are supposed to be in each moment and each subsequent moment. We do not need to strive or try to be somewhere else or someone else; we are perfect the way we are.

The universe is not inherently flawed, and nothing in the universe is inherently flawed. If we look at a tree, for instance, we may see knots in the trunk. The knots do not mean the tree is flawed. If we focus on the knots we may think the tree is imperfect, but what we miss is the wholeness of the tree and the beauty of the creation. All we have to do is allow ourselves to see the beauty of it all—to see where we fit into the All-That-Is, and recognize the beauty contained in our "knots." Ironically, it is what we consider our flaws that make us unique, as each design in a mosaic is unique. In this uniqueness we are perfect, as is the mosaic.

We are spiritual beings experiencing the dimension of humanity simultaneously with the spiritual dimension. We are connected to the Source or Creator - The All-That-Is lives within and around all of us in every moment.

All movement and actions of the universe are interconnected and are in complete harmony and balance. The universe is endless and contains all possibilities. There is room for all human actions and movements to be in harmony and balance within the entire unfoldment of the universe. There are no exceptions. What appears to be imbalance and disharmony is merely the result of our perceptions that miss the wholeness and purpose of the actions and movement. It is not important that we know the purpose; it is important that we know there is purpose.

The unfoldment of the universe is not random, nor is it predestined. This means that all movement and actions are spontaneous in each moment. If we believe there is predestination and that the Creator has everything mapped out for us, we have limited the Creator and its intelligence to create and recreate in each moment.

We are free to choose what we want to do. If we realize the intelligence of the universe and our connection to it, all we need do is to get out of our own way to be free to live in happiness. It is there. It is only we who think it is not.

Free Will

Our free will to choose is based on two types of choices: those based in love and those based in fear. Love is all there is. It is what holds the warmth and beauty of the universe together, like glue. Fear is an illusion that is chosen by the ego. Essentially, when we make choices, love is always present when we surrender to what is and remain in the choice of love. Any other action chooses fear. By surrendering to what is we choose to live with Essence as one and to find our way back home to Essence or love. Ironically, when we experience it, we realize that we already are home and always have been. There is no other place to go; it is all one.

Choosing either way—to stay in love or fear—is part of the universal plan because there is no separation or anything outside of the universe. To say that fear is not of the universe is to make it separate, and it is not. Illusion is part of the universe. There is room for all possibilities. Regardless of our choices, the universe always remains in perfect balance and harmony. We can choose to surrender to it or to go kicking and screaming in fear. We may say that we are all on the roller coaster ride of life. There are those who bend with the twists and turns and those who hang on, white-knuckled with fear, resisting the twists and turns as if they think they have the strength to do so. Nevertheless, we all are on the same ride; the difference is the choice between loving it and fearing it. Choices made through fear cause suffering because they are based on the false belief that there is separation between Essence and ourselves.

Fear creates choices that are based on the five physical senses and are discordant with the movement and flow of the universe. Ego creates the illusion that we are separate and our actions do not affect the universe—that our actions cause something to happen that is separate from the universe. This negates unity and is the basis for cause and effect. It is like saying that the actions of the waves in the ocean affect only what is around them and not the entire ocean. The belief that our actions affect only one thing and not another is a belief in separation. In the mosaic example, it is like saying that each pattern in the mosaic is separate from the whole pattern and that because it is separate, it does not affect the entire mosaic. If we change a pattern in the mosaic, the entire image of the mosaic changes.

Change occurs constantly. At a micro level, we see that all things change. At a macro level, we see that nothing changes. However, any change alters everything else because the universe is unified and total in itself. There are no separations or seams - when one thing appears to change, the entire whole changes.

When we make choices based on fear, which are generated at the egoic levels, we choose to cling to the energy of experiences and assign meaning to them. There are no meanings to events except for the meanings we assign to them, which are based on past events or future hopes. When we cling to energy, we hold it in on a cellular level. We restrict its natural

flow and use enormous amounts of energy to cling to
these experiences. It is like saying we came into this
life with 100 units of life energy, and then chose to
use 30 units of this energy to hold onto events to
which we have assigned some meaning. When we do
this we are not operating on all cylinders,
experiencing the wonderment and beauty of creation.
We evaluate everything we experience based on
judgment and comparison to the past rather than
experiencing it on our own. Buddhists have an idea
they call "keeping your cup empty," which means
that whenever we fill our cups, we need to empty
them in order to fill them up again. This allows us to
experience anew every event in every moment, and to
see the wonder in it.

Choosing to remain in love is for the best and
highest good of the universe, through spiritual
consciousness. It is immortal and eternal. Choosing
fear is for what we <u>think</u> is our highest good within
the limitations of being human. It is mortal and
limited.

Present Moment

Existence is a succession of moments. The
universe is so intelligent that the succession of
moments is created and recreated in each moment.
The universal unfoldment is not dependent on the
past or the future; it is spontaneous. Since there is a
succession of created moments, the universe is in
perfect unfoldment within the universal plan. When
we choose to hold onto energy from past experiences
or for future hopes, we fail to see that there is a plan

greater than ours. It is important to us to know there is a universal plan, but it is not important that we know what that plan is. This is called faith. There exists only a now presence, and each moment contains a new now presence as the universe unfolds.

Our perceptions of reality limit our focus. What we focus on becomes real through our perceptions. Fear focus fixates on specific areas in which we assign meaning to events. This focus is connected to our false core beliefs: not being who we truly are because we think we are not good enough—that we are flawed—and as a result of being ourselves, we will be abandoned. With the ego out of balance and filtering our focus, it generates energy so that we cling to the false core beliefs. Because we hold on to these thoughts, we feel guilt and shame. Guilt is thinking we are separate from everything else and that we did something wrong. Shame is the belief that at the core, we are flawed. We cling so tightly to the energies of guilt and shame that they seem normal and are buried in the unconscious, repressed from consciousness.

These repressed feelings are so deep that we have created our perceptions of life through their filters. We then project them outward onto other people and things, and cast blame for our unhappiness or dissatisfaction. Projection is the unconscious screaming for attention, screaming out to be recognized. It demands attention because the unconscious knows it is not in our best interests to cling to these energies; it wants to be reunited with consciousness. Within this screaming is truth.

Projection is an unconscious focus of how we feel about ourselves, judge ourselves, and compare ourselves to others. Projection puts us into victim energy, which means we think that someone, something, or God has hurt us, and as a result, we are stuck in the victim consciousness mode. In *Radical Forgiveness,* Colin Tipping notes, " 'Seen from a spiritual standpoint, our pain and discomfort in any given situation provide a signal that we are out of alignment with spiritual law and are being given an opportunity to heal something. This may be some original pain or perhaps a toxic belief that stops us from becoming our true selves. We don't often see a situation from this perspective, however. Rather, we judge the situation and blame others for what is happening, which prevents us from seeing the message or understanding in the lesson.' " [9]

The law of resonance says that we emit or project energy out into the world. This energy draws in people and situations that resonate with it. Because we get back what we send out, we attract people and situations that mirror our projections so that we may see what we are projecting and do something about it. It is universal grace seeking the best and highest good: for energy to move freely and for us to evolve and heal victim energy. It always happens and is always present in the moment. The Creator does not give us more than we can handle in each moment, which makes each moment precious for the development of the soul.

---

[9] Colin Tipping, *Radical Forgiveness,* 17.

Mirroring back to us what we project outwardly triggers the guilt and shame we hide inside. We need to recognize the truth contained in it and reconcile it by letting go of the energy blockages and the issues connected to them. There is no other way than to experience the truth of the issues connected to guilt and shame. What we find is that mirrors show us things that were taken from us, or that we lost or gave away. These losses create perceived holes in ourselves that we choose to fill with fear fixations. What was lost, stolen, or given away is all connected to love and the highest and best purpose of the universe, if we are courageous enough to see them. Colin Tipping in, *Radical Forgiveness,* writes, "To transform something, we must be able to experience it completely and fully. To transform the victim archetype, we must fully experience victimhood. No shortcut exists."[10] (Note: We recommend this book for a complete and detailed process through forgiveness.)

Real forgiveness is allowing repressed feelings to surface, experiencing the truth contained in them, and allowing them to lead us back to what was always there: love. This allows energy to flow, and the energy we used to hold and cling to dissipate. This transforms victim (negative) energy to divine love energy. It reconnects the consciousness with the unconsciousness and allows evolvement of our soul through spirituality according to perfection, universal laws, and natural unfoldment. It is living life on all cylinders.

---

[10] Ibid, 2.

Real Forgiveness Assumptions

Multi-sensory – Real forgiveness is a high vibrational alignment with the best and highest good of the universe. It is the source of divine love, and is not ego-centered or driven by ego. It concerns itself with unblocking repressed energy and allowing it to flow through us.

Nonjudgmental – Real forgiveness transcends the duality of right/wrong or victim/perpetrator. It recognizes the perfection in the universal plan and natural unfoldment. It acknowledges that nothing wrong happened to us; everything that happened was part of the universal dance.

Mirrors – Real forgiveness understands and sees the feelings associated with repressed memories and the emotions attached to them. It knows that what comes back to us is what we project outwardly—symbols of what was lost, stolen, or given away. Our projections reveal the ways in which we judged ourselves to be insufficient by what we perceived as lost, stolen, or given away.

There are two ways of spreading light: to be the candle, or the mirror that reflects it. —Edith Wharton

Transformation - Real forgiveness is an internal, not external, transformation of energy. We do not forgive someone else for "doing something wrong" to us. We forgive and let go of the energy attached to the duality of victim/perpetrator. Thinking that forgiveness is forgiving someone else assumes that we are right and they are wrong. Regardless of our perceptions of right and wrong, assuming rightness and wrongness places us in a state of arrogant righteousness, which is egoic. We miss the point of universal unfoldment and the perfection of all that occurs.

Universal - It is the universe that truly forgives; we do not. Thinking that we do is thinking that we control it and know what is right and wrong, which is vain and egoic. The source of all forgiveness is higher vibration—more complex patterns. It is surrendering to the unfoldment and perfection of the universe and aligning ourselves with it.

Change – Real forgiveness does not require that something be changed. It is allowing and accepting of what happened as it was, just the way it was.

Unconditional – Real forgiveness is unconditional—there are no limits or exceptions. Any limits or exceptions create energy blockages and are egoic.

An example of real forgiveness:

I was raised in a home that was violent. I saw my father beat my mother and sisters, and felt the brutality of his blows on my body. My mother also was violent, but her blows were not as sharp as my father's. I learned that I was not good enough as I was, and altered myself to please my parents. I developed a sense of self-protection by reacting before thinking. This is Enneatype Eight energy.

Going through life, I was on my guard. I pushed people away from me and would not let them get close because I was afraid of being hurt. I am able to expand my energy so that it seems as though my boundaries are in the next county.

When I was 25 years old, I moved away from my family and set up my life across the country. I thought it was their fault that I was miserable and my life was not going in the direction I expected it to go. I was unhappy and blamed them for it—I became a victim. I divorced myself from my parents, felt ashamed that they were my family, and did not contact them again for a long time.

Throughout my life, people and situations constantly mirrored back to me the energy I held, the victim energy I used as an excuse not to be who I truly am. I wondered how there could be a God when these things happened to me, and believed that there was only pain and violence in this world. I thought warmth and love did not exist, and that the way through life was to turn off feelings and gut it out like a man.

One day I stopped and reflected on the energy that was returning to me. It always came back, no matter what I did: hypnosis, *meditation, affirmations, and energy alignments. They were only temporary and did nothing to change the way I felt about myself. I allowed the energy to arise and I saw it for what it really was. I realized that I was the one who took part of myself and clung to the energy that kept me from living live in its fullest splendor. I regained love. It was always there, even when I thought it was not.*

When the universal love energy flowed through me, I was able to transform the hate, resentment, guilt, and shame I had for my parents into unconditional love and acceptance for what happened, just the way it happened.

I called my parents for the first time in sixteen years and told them I loved them and wanted to communicate with them again. I did not expect them to change; I didn't even expect them to respond after all of those years. What I did was for my growth, and to let them know how much love I had for them. It did not matter to me if they responded positively; it was not important. What was important was that I said what I had to say from my heart and soul.

There was a complete transformation, because they did respond to my heart. To this day, I have had a very loving relationship with my parents. They did not change; they did not have to. I changed, and now I am happy.

The Enneatypes and Forgiveness

Since we have taken on personality types and within those types, aligned ourselves with egoic fixations, what can we do to transform the fixated energy patterns into those of real forgiveness? As energy flows through the Enneagram structure, we are faced with choices to continue moving in the direction of the Path of Disintegration (Stress Point), which furthers our fixations. Alternately, we can realize the perfection and unfoldment of the energy, bring it forth, see it for what it really is, reconcile it, and then automatically move forward through the Path of Integration (Heart Point). We use the term "automatically" because once repressed fear energy is freed, we align with the love that has always been there and was blocked by our choice to live in ego-related fear.

For example, if we create a scenario leading Enneatype Eight through the Path of Disintegration, it may flow as follows: The Eight pushes outwardly and assertively in the environment. His purpose is to create large, expansive, and lustful energy boundaries to prevent other people from posing a threat to him. To an Eight, the best defense is a formidable offense, and he bullies people in an attempt to control them. Under stress, he moves more and more assertively against people until they revolt and in doing so violate the Eight's boundaries, and threaten his safety.

When experiencing undue stress, Eights move to the Stress Point of Five. They withdraw to lick their wounds and plan ways to get even and exact revenge. Unless Eights see the truth of why they were fixated, they will start to disintegrate. Continuing disintegration may occur as Eights experience more stress and move to the Five's Stress Point of Seven. There, Eights become gluttonous and experience multiple activities incessantly to keep them from thinking about their feelings and the pain they feel. When they find that this behavior cannot quell the pain, they may move to the Stress Point of Seven, the One. At the One point, Eights restrain themselves and try to repress anger and rage by lashing out at others, being sarcastic, and preaching what others should and should not do. This strategy may have the effect of pushing people away from them, and may propel Eights to the Stress Point of One, the Four. Feeling that others do not appreciate them, they withdraw, become moody, and fantasize about what is missing in their lives. This creates envy. They project outwardly and blame those around them for their misery. Realizing that withdrawal and emoting does not ease their pain, they may move to the Stress Point of Four, the Two. At the Two, Eights move toward others, realizing that they need other people and trying to get people to need them. Eights attempt to show others how important they are to them. This strategy creates pride. As people move away from the manipulation, Eights at Two may become more stressed and move to the Stress Point of Two, the Eight. Here, Eights begin the circle again.

Ironically, Two is the Heart Point of Eight, and Eights can move there through the Path of Integration. Moving there through disintegration and stress, however, creates behaviors at the unevolved or lower end of the types. At any time, the Eight in this example could have moved along the circumference of the Enneagram to the primary points of Nine, Three, and Six. Here they would have experienced the unevolved behaviors of these types. Also, at any time, Eights can fixate within their own Stress Point and develop antisocial behaviors associated with Eights (such as murder).

This example is a possible scenario that is not limited to Eights. Every Enneatype has the ability to move from point to point. To state otherwise would limit possibilities and limit people in probable behavior and energy movements. The traditional Enneagram addresses probabilities that work on most occasions. When we are dealing with people, we need to recognize the possibilities of behavior and be prepared to deal with them. Also, it should be noted that although each type moves from point to point, at its core, the egoic fixation of the original type remains. Fear manifests fear. Ego manipulates the fear so it seems as though we are changing, but that is a deception of ego, an illusion of the ego making us think we are evolving. We cannot evolve through fear. We can evolve only by releasing fear, seeing its truth, and returning to the original state of love.

If we strive for spirituality and consciously move in the direction of the Path of Integration (Heart Point) we will not achieve it. Doing so would indicate that the ego has directed us to do this. The ego cannot lead us in a spiritual direction because its own survival would be at stake. Ego does not want us to realize spirituality because ego believes in separation, while our spiritual nature understands universal unity. Ego may trick us into thinking we are striving toward spirituality by setting us up for failure—again. Ego will delude us into focusing on our fixations; thus, spirituality is viewed through egoic filters, the same perceptions that put us there in the first place. In these events, ego wears different clothes. What difference does it make how ego controls us? What difference does it make if we transform one fixation for another? We are deluded into thinking that we are healing by striving to be one with the universe and tapping into spirituality. We try to meditate, we try to pray, we try to make ourselves understand beauty and wonderment, or we try any New Age fad-of-the-month, hoping to attain spiritual awareness.

When we move consciously to the Heart Points, typical behavior for each Enneatype is as follows: the One tries to loosen up and make himself have fun; the Two tries to make herself reflect on her own needs; the Three tries to slow down and become a team player; the Four tries to become serious and self-disciplined; the Five tries to come out of his shell and be present in the moment; the Six tries to slow down and think she is safe in her body and the environment; the Seven tries to slow down, become more reflective, and glean more meaning from experiences; the Eight tries to become philanthropic and do things for others; and the Nine tries to wake up and go into action doing meaningful things.

If we try to make it happen, we negate the spontaneous flow of universal energy. We say that we are in charge and can control our spiritual growth. This is not surrender; it is not letting go of repressed energy. It is arrogance, vanity, deceit, pride, and denial. It is thinking we can recognize our repressed energy with our heads, know what course we should take, and try to connect with it. It is another lie of the ego. If we have to try to be ourselves, we can never be ourselves.

Authors have developed distinctions between the Path of Integration (Heart Point) and the Security Point. In *The Wisdom of the Enneagram,* Riso and Hudson note that going to the Security Point is when an average level Enneatype acts out by trying to mimic the behavior of the Enneatype at the Heart Point. Acting out is acting out, regardless of the direction. It is still striving to be someone other than who we really are, or striving to be what ego makes us think we really are.

Regarding the Direction of Integration, Riso and Hudson say, ". . . it is the ego's way of automatically compensating for imbalances in our psyches. Transformation in the Direction of Integration is another matter, however, because moving in the Direction of Integration requires conscious choice." [11] The person chooses to be fully alive and present in life—to awaken and follow a path leading to wholeness by surrendering to the universe.

Hurley and Donson, in *Enneagram for the 21st Century,* write, "Why do the 'arrows' [Heart Points], which are in part supposed to show you a path for growth and transformation, point you toward a type with a similar problem (the same preferred center) for the Two and the Seven? Why do arrows attempt to describe transformation by emulating the 'high side'

---

[11] Riso and Hudson, *The Wisdom of the Enneagram,* 91.

of another type when even the high side of a compulsion is still a compulsion?"[12] They go on to note that once we recognize the compulsion, we still must figure out what to do about it.

We are suggesting that to go into any conscious direction, we need to wake up and become aware of the behaviors that led us to compulsions. We must be able to recognize that we are unhappy not being our true selves. This is very difficult to do, but it is a start. Ego in its nature has made us blind. It lies to us as it controls and filters our perceptions, making us think we are on a path of healing when ego is in charge. How can that be? How can we truly manifest our real selves when we are striving to be the person we already are? How can we try to live in love when love is buried in repressed feelings that we created? How can we try to live in love when we are already there but do not see it?

The Enneatypes have fixated on issues that prevent them from manifesting their true natures. At some point, we gave away who we truly are. We developed compulsions based on what was lost or given away. What was lost and given away creates reactions to what is mirrored back to us, which trigger the repressed feelings that make us cling to energy rather than allowing it to flow spontaneously and naturally. Recognition of these energies, allowing them to surface, and reconciling them for what they really are automatically drives us in true Paths of Integration. These paths are internal and unique to

---

[12] Hurley and Donson, *Enneagram for the 21st Century,* 3.

every one of us; they are our paths. On these paths
we experience real forgiveness, which is complete and
healing in itself.

Enneagram Projections and Mirrors

Type	Lost or Taken away	Mirror / Reaction
One	Perfection	Criticism / Judgment
Two	Self-worth	Neediness
Three	Authenticity	Striving
Four	Connection	Special / Unique
Five	Intelligence	Withdrawal
Six	Faith / Courage	Cynicism
Seven	Nurturing	Immaturity
Eight	Innocence	Revenge
Nine	Significance	Inferiority

Each Enneatype, through the energy of what
was lost, given away, or taken away, creates the
delusion of victim consciousness. Victim
consciousness occurs when we think something

wrong has been done to us. We cling to this energy, looking for ways to compensate for the loss. (Each Enneatype does this differently.) This creates reactions, which are mirrors of how we react to what was lost. Every time we present these behaviors, people and situations remind us of what was lost or given away and mirror them back to us. This dynamic occurs because we are fully focused on the fixations that drive these behaviors.

Below is a description how each Enneatype mimics this behavior and what can be done to transform it.

One: The Perfectionist – We all are born in universal perfection. Since the All-That-Is is the Creator, there is nothing out of place: everything and every event are perfect within its own essence.

Ones learned that they were not good enough the way they were and that to be accepted, they had to be "good little boys/girls." In order to be good, they had to meet someone else's standards of perfection. To achieve someone else's standards of perfection means that perfection is not inherent, thus it is outside of us. Since it is external, inherent perfection is lost or given away, and Ones begin to strive for external approval, thinking that they are inherently flawed and not worthy of unconditional love. Striving for relative perfection retards spontaneity and natural rhythmic flow. Internally, anger from not being oneself is repressed, creating rigidity within the body. Ones become victims of relative perfectionism by chasing it and never living the absolute perfection of the universe.

They focus their perceptions on relative perfection: what is right and what is wrong, what is moral and what is immoral, and what is good and what is bad. They see the world as fitting into only one part of the duality, and judge the world as they judge themselves: based on a relative standard of perfection. Ones have intense and incessant inner critics—the voice inside that reminds them of how they should act to be good. This is a judgment on how they are. When their inner critics judge them, Ones project this criticism out onto the world. They constantly judge people and situations based on their way of seeing perfection, and compulsively compare themselves and others through these egoic filters. Mirroring criticism back to them, Ones feel anger and resentment build inside, and they question their ideals.

Ones find forgiveness by understanding the anger driving their inner critics. They need to experience the feeling of not being good enough just the way they are, which is done by allowing anger to arise and seeing the truth that they were not loved for who they really were. They must realize that there is relative perfection and inherent perfection, and that inherent perfection is within everything, everyone, and every situation.

Two: The Giver – Everyone is born with needs: we need to be nourished and to live in love. Whenever we experience that the only way to be nourished and loved is through nourishing and loving other people, we learn that others are more important than we are and that their needs take precedence over ours.

Twos learned to take care of their parents, siblings, relatives, and/or friends. They learned that by doing so, they received attention. When other people depend on us, we find that we are needed, and in that need, we may feel love. This is false love. As long as we take care of others, we think that we are loved not for who we are, but for what we do for them. This is conditional, and love is not conditional. Twos take care of others and try to get others to need them, yet they believe that they do not need help from others; thus, pride develops. Twos believe they became victims by thinking that their needs are secondary or that they have no needs except to get others to need them. Believing that their needs are secondary creates a lack of real self-worth, and they feel they are not good enough.

Twos focus their attention on doing whatever they can do for other people. They thrive on getting attention by having other people need them. Twos live for the pleasure of others and will change themselves to meet the needs of others. The compulsive drive to get other people to need us is called neediness, and this is what Twos project out onto the world. Mirrored back to them, neediness triggers repressed memories of not being nourished and loved for themselves. When Twos feel unneeded, anger, shame, and humiliation surface through wounded pride. They project blame on others, trying to make them feel ungrateful.

Twos find forgiveness by seeing that their needs are as important as anyone else's needs. In fact, they may find that if their own needs were met, they would not act compulsively to meet the needs of others. Meeting one's own needs first builds self-worth. When we meet our own needs, we are better at meeting the needs of others because we are connected to real needs, understand what they are, and develop compassion for others and ourselves. Twos need to feel the pain and shame of not being good enough to have their own needs met when they were children. Seeing the pain for what it really is, and reconciling it, they fill themselves with nourishment from the universe.

Three: The Performer – Everything in the universe is authentic and genuine, as real and genuine as spirit. We are born connected to the All-That-Is, and are always connected to it. There is a natural flow in the movement of the universe within fixed physical laws. We do not have to add to it, subtract from it, or do anything different from the natural flow. All we have to be is ourselves.

When Threes were children, they learned that they did not get attention and love for whom they were, and that love and attention were present only when they did something, when they achieved some type of goal that pleased their parents. They were valued as people for their achievements. As a result, Threes learned that they had to <u>do</u>—they had to accomplish things and look good at doing so. Doing things to get attention, love, and self-worth implies that without the doing, we would be worthless and unlovable. Thus, vanity arises. Vanity is thinking we are separate from All-That-Is and have to do because we do not trust that the Creator will guide us. Looking good at achieving means that we feel we have to change ourselves to meet what we think are others' expectations in order to get attention from them. This belief deprives us of authenticity and genuineness. Losing authenticity, we deceive others and ourselves about who we really are. In deceit, Threes lost themselves and believe they became victims.

Threes focus their perceptions on performance and achievements. They see the world as rewarding those who perform the most efficiently and with the approval of others. They judge themselves by their accomplishments. When others approve of them, they are given job promotions and opportunities to achieve even more. To the outside world, Threes project striving; they typically are seen as striving for something else. Mirroring striving back to Threes triggers that they are not accepted for who they are. They may think that who they are is what they do, but this is just self-deception.

Threes find forgiveness by understanding that they do not have to make things happen. They can be accepted for the content of their characters, not by what they accomplish. Their striving is compulsive because nothing they accomplish outside of themselves has depth enough to satisfy their burning desire to be loved for who they are. Ego provides the delusion that self-worth lies in doing. As truth arises and is recognized and reconciled, Threes transform themselves by slowing down and allowing themselves to act within the natural flow of universal energy.

Four: The Romantic – Everything and everyone in the universe is connected—not only horizontally, but also connected vertically to Source. The universe is seamless and moving as one; there are no exceptions.

As children, Fours felt abandoned. They believed they would not have been abandoned if they had been worthy, if they were not inherently flawed. Not only did Fours feel abandoned by someone close to them, they felt abandoned by the Creator. Thus, they lost their connection with the Source, the Universe, the All-That-Is. Thinking we are separated from Source creates emotions of melancholy. Fours believe they became ultimate victims by the loss of connection with Source, which makes them feel that they are separate from everything and everybody else. Fours see other people as being happy while they are miserable, which creates envy. Feeling disconnected while everyone else is happy results in Fours believing that they are special and unique because they are alienated and abandoned.

Fours focus their perceptions on being different and unique. They strive to reconnect by developing relationships that fill the emotional void of being abandoned, which is an attempt to get external gratification to compensate for what is missing inside. They think they deserve a person who will come along and save them, and try to mold themselves into someone unique—someone other than who they truly are—hoping that the "knight on a white horse" will appear. They project this energy onto the world. Mirroring separate uniqueness back to Fours triggers intense emotional pain, as feelings of abandonment and separation surface. Feeling inherently flawed through disconnection causes shame.

Fours find forgiveness by understanding that Essence was always with them and never abandoned them. They discover that it was they who abandoned themselves, and realize that they are unique and special, as is everyone else. They tap into the unique spiritual gifts they were born with. Fours need to allow the truth of envy, pain, and abandonment to surface, experience this truth for what it really is, and reconcile it.

Five: The Observer – The universe is highly intelligent. In fact, the universe contains all the intelligence that ever was and ever will exist. By tapping into universal intelligence, we realize all the intelligence we need is present in any given moment. Fives were nagged and pressured and had to find their own privacy, their own little world where they could have time to think. They withdrew. They learned that they received attention and love based upon how much knowledge they acquired, because knowledge helped them figure out the world. Fives were urged to study hard and receive good grades in school. This strategy provided a level of conditional love: love for being knowledgeable.

By giving up themselves, Fives lost the connection to universal intelligence. Universal intelligence is the knowing that there is infinite knowledge available at any moment through connection with the universe. In losing universal intelligence, Fives believe they became victims. To

Fives, intelligence is cerebral. When they interface with the world and people, they need time and space to figure out how they feel about it. In this way, they withdraw into their cerebral realities. They do this so compulsively that they are willing to give up material comforts and time with their families to have this time, thus they develop avarice of energy.

Fives focus their perceptions through cerebral knowledge. They see the world as logical, a place where they can sit alone and figure it out. When they cannot figure it out, they assume they lack the knowledge necessary to do so. This pushes them into further withdrawal to learn more. Withdrawal projects inadequacy to handle reality in the present moment. Mirrored back to Fives, withdrawal triggers loneliness and emptiness, feelings of inadequacy for handling real life.

Fives find forgiveness by feeling the adequacy of present energy. By shutting down and freezing out people, they not only erect walls to keep out others, but the walls keep Fives inside. As truth arises and Fives see that they already possess all the knowledge they need in the moment, they will reconcile the energy surrounding the impoverishment and inadequacy. They become present and live fully in each moment.

Six: The Doubter – Faith is a deep knowing that God exists and is our inner nature; it is not a belief in a particular system, religion, or person. Sixes were raised in environments that promoted fear. They felt that they were not loved for who they were, because to be who they were generated some type of punishment related to fear. In giving up themselves, Sixes either lost faith or had it taken away from them. They learned that God was not within their inner natures, that they were inherently flawed and had to search for Source elsewhere. Sixes experienced the world as being unsafe and felt that they would not be supported and were in constant danger. Thus, they became doubters of not only the existence of Essence, but also the fact that Essence is inherent in each of us. Sixes believe they became victims by losing their safety and security, which launched them on a constant search for safety. They look for safety externally in people, religions, "isms," and organizations.

Sixes focus their perceptions on fear, resulting in insecurity and searching for a means of safety. External searching implies that we are afraid of what we may see inside. We believe we are inherently flawed and that the environment is dangerous, imperfect, and bad. Losing courage for inward journeys, we project fear and cynicism outwardly. Cynicism doubts our inner nature, and in that doubting, there is a doubting of God. Cynicism mirrored back to Sixes triggers anxiety related to their safety and causes great stress as they move around anxiously looking for support.

Sixes find forgiveness in realizing that they were not loved for who they were, and that harm came to them whenever they tried to be themselves. This created their fear of the environment. As fear arises through cynicism, they can experience the pain in what they had taken from them: safety. As truth is experienced and reconciled, Sixes reestablish their faith and find comfort and serenity in knowing and trusting the universe.

Seven: The Epicure – Everyone needs nurturing. When we are children we need to be fed, clothed, changed, held, and loved for who we are. Parents are needed to encourage their children to manifest the gifts they were born with. When nurturing is insufficient or missing, we respond internally, keeping ourselves occupied to avoid feeling the pain associated with this lack.

Seven children had to learn to nurture themselves. When children try to nurture themselves, they cannot do so at mature levels. What is actually happening is a substitution for the real thing, a false, and pseudo-nurturing. What Sevens lost was real nurturing. They developed substitutions in their heads. They incessantly plan and engage in activities that keep them numb from the loss of primal nurturing. Gluttony (incessant, superficial activity) is a result. Sevens believe they became victims as they gave up being themselves because they were not nurtured sufficiently.

Sevens focus their perceptions on planning and activities to dull inner reality. Excessive planning and engaging in relentless activities project immaturity onto the world. Sevens are like children who go from activity to activity, never stopping to fully enjoy and focus on the depth of experience (similar to Attention Deficit Disorder). They believe quantity is more important than quality. Although Sevens may argue that they are interested in cultural activities such as the symphony, theater, fine dining, and art, and may equate these activities with depth, they usually are picky, superficial, and dilettantish.

Planning is going through the motions, believing there is no divine Plan, so we think we must plan instead of going with the energy flow of the universal plan. Immaturity is mirrored back to Sevens and triggers the emptiness inside that resulted from insufficient nurturing. They retreat and feel repressed, unmet needs that are expressed through irritation, sarcasm, and increased activities as their minds go into overdrive.

Sevens find forgiveness by realizing that real nurturing was lost, which left deep holes that they tried to fill with activities. Their pseudo-nurturing only substituted for the real thing. The pain of deprivation surfaces, and needs to be felt and reconciled for what it really is. As truth is experienced and reconciled, Sevens slow down and experience the depth of life as they regain internal nurturing.

Eight: The Boss – Violence begets violence. Martin Luther King, Jr. said, "The old law about 'an eye for an eye' leaves everybody blind." Children need to feel secure in their environment. Many Eight children grew up in violent homes and learned to defend themselves by reacting before they could think. They learned that the strong dominate and control the weak. Reacting to violence, Eights needed excessive energy and strength to survive, which created lust. Children raised in this type of environment give up or lost the safety and security of innocence. Losing innocence, they must always remain on edge and in control. Eights realized they were not accepted for the innocence of who they were. They changed by repressing their feelings and becoming aggressive, outwardly attacking and looking for ways to avenge their pain by pushing out onto the environment.

Eights focus their perceptions on extreme behavior, lustfully seeking safety and security. Pushing against the environment, Eights try to control people, events, situations, and themselves. They project energy outwardly, trying to get others to do and act as they think they should. When others rebel against intrusive Eights, the Eights retreat and look for ways to exact revenge. This energy of vengeance that is mirrored back to Eights triggers the original pain of the loss of safety and security of innocence. Revenge is a way of attempting to heal by hurting others, trying in vain to regain the original state of lost innocence.

Eights find forgiveness by allowing the pain from the loss of innocence to arise from the gut. As truth is experienced and reconciled, Eights open their feelings and find compassion and empathy for others. They learn that the best control is no control. The universe is perfectly balanced and in harmony just the way it is.

Nine: The Mediator – Existence is filled with wonder and beauty. Everything and everyone in the universe is in the right place at the right time. There is no need to add to it or take away from it. Existence is warm and good, and always going in the direction of blissful unfoldment. Since the universe is one, everything and everyone is significant. The Creator imbued each of us with divine gifts.

As children, Nines were raised in environments that promoted their insignificance. They felt they could not be who they really are because their true self was not accepted by their significant others, so they learned to merge with other people in an attempt to make themselves significant. Nines fall asleep to whom they truly are. They believe they became victims by trying to change and mold themselves into someone who would be accepted. They learned that love was conditional and they were not lovable; they were inherently flawed and inferior.

Nines think they are responsible for maintaining peace and harmony in and around them. They lost the concept that peace and harmony already exist at all times in the universe. To maintain peace and harmony, Nines merge with others and shut themselves down emotionally. They become indolent.

Nines focus their perceptions on merging with others so that they do not have to be responsible for any outcomes. To maintain peace and harmony, they avoid inner feelings that may disturb peace, and try to escape from reality. Universal peace and harmony exist at all times; there is no effort required to feel it internally. Looking for peace and harmony externally, Nines need to merge with others. They project insignificance of self onto other people by seeing all options as neutral. That is, they think that when decisions are to be made and something needs to be done, all options have the same amount of significance. They do not know how to prioritize their choices because they believe they lack significance within themselves. They project looking for a life, looking for significance, and someone other than the self they feel they lost. When inferiority is mirrored back to them, it triggers the feeling of loss of themselves, causing guilt, resentment, and anger.

Nines find forgiveness in experiencing the anger as it arises, seeing the truth within, and reconciling it. They realize that they are loved and are significant, that their feelings and opinions are important, and that they do have their own lives and choices.

18 Compassion: The Result of Understanding

If you want others to be happy, practice compassion. If you want to be happy, practice compassion. —Dalai Lama

As we integrate ourselves and become more loving, caring, and forgiving, we move to another level of humanness: a level at which we become compassion. It is a level that exists in every moment and can be achieved by all of us through transformation of self. Compassion is something we become, not something we choose to do when we feel like doing it. Compassion, then, is not connected to conscious action, as in thinking, "Today I will be compassionate." It is something we manifest throughout our entire Being, something we live in each moment.

Compassion extends beyond words, encompassing Being in its entirety as a state of unity. It is a merging of the entire being into the All-That–Is. Compassion manifested through Being creates presence in the moment; being in the moment creates internal drive in love.

The universe, in its infinite wisdom, allows us to freely choose what we want to manifest, regardless of that choice. There is no judgment of the choice. This is why if we want to destroy the earth by raping its resources, destroying the plants and forests that allow us to breathe, and dumping tons of chemicals and pollutants into our water supply, so be it. Who pays the price for this? If we want to kill each other in wars over who controls resources, then so be it. If we choose dysfunctional behavior and move ourselves perceptually away from the loving source, then so be it. Who suffers? We do. The universe may be said to be compassionate in these events because compassion negates judgment—it is experiencing life without filters and judgments. It is accepting what is, as it is, with no changes.

Judgment is a sense of rightness and wrongness and is dependent on the point of view of who is judging. It is attached to projection of the things that were lost, given away, or taken away from us. When we are judging, we are projecting. Judgment embraces and needs duality. From a spiritual point of view, there is no duality. It is all One: the All-That-Is. Duality keeps us trapped in the illusion that we are separate from the source. If we are to move to the level of compassion, then we must be able to integrate duality and experience the relevance of it through a universal viewpoint. We must experience life without attachment to outcomes and expectations. When we experience life with expected outcomes to events, we limit ourselves to those outcomes and miss other opportunities presented in the moment. If we are expecting the outcome to be "A", we may miss the possibilities contained in outcomes, "B-Z". Expecting outcomes and not achieving them creates emotional attachments that may lead to fixations.

The free-flowing, boundless energy of the universe allows our thoughts, feelings, and emotions to create energy fixations, and alters vibrations that empower whatever we focus on. If we focus on the things that destroy us, then the energy vibrations alter and give us more of those things. There is a universal law that says, "What we resist, persists." Resistance to what is traps energy inside us. We use energy to accomplish this and because we do, the natural flow of energy alters. If we resist internal anger, we use energy to try to control it, and perhaps deny that we are angry. We assume we should not be angry, and this assumption implies that we should know how to feel or how not to feel. This reaction enhances the energy charge (emotion) associated with repressed anger because we judged ourselves on how we should feel. We feel the way we feel. Holding onto anger is resistance to what is. It generates feelings and emotions that, if repressed, escalate into rage, envy, and resentment. Resistance to what is creates further empowerment of that which we cling to.

The universe is like a big photocopy machine: what we give away always comes back to us because the universe thinks we need to replenish it, and does this in its splendor and perfection. This is the universe in non-judgment of our actions. If we give away hatred, bias, and violence, this is what we get in return. If we give away love, forgiveness, and compassion, this is what we get in return. In a way, we may call this free will. We reap what we sow.

In the previous chapter on forgiveness, we learned that forgiveness releases attachment to compulsive meanings of events and assists us in realizing truth. In truth, we live through unity, purpose, and love. Healing from inside, we then project into the environment those traits needed to live with God and love. Through this, without judgment and attachment, we allow and accept what is to be. When this projected energy returns to us, our perceptions are clear and unbiased, and our mirrors reflect this clarity.

In the Enneagram, and in the discussion of forgiveness, we found that the truths lost, given away, or taken away from us were Perfection, Self-Worth, Authenticity, Connection with Source, Intelligence, Faith Courage, Nurturance, Innocence, and Significance. Forgiveness restores all these truths and allows us to move to compassion. Compassion reveals additional truths that are learned through experiencing who we really are, using the Enneagram as a tool.

Truths of Compassion

Warmth – The universe moves and changes as the unfoldment of consciousness changes from one unified field to another. This unfoldment is in accordance with fixed universal laws, and within it is intelligence that is warm and loving. Knowing that there is warmth in the unfoldment, we learn to trust ourselves just the way we are, without judgment. We know that there is warmth in the environment and we will be taken care of if we allow the energy to flow naturally. If we let go and allow for spontaneity, we will harmonize with universal unfoldment. The energy of the universe flows within its own truth, and that truth, like water, always seeks its own level. By allowing truth to surface, we free ourselves.

For well you know that it's a fool that plays it cool by making this world a little colder. —The Beatles

Openness – When relating to others and ourselves, we need to be honest and open. In openness, we do not need to defend our actions because there is nothing we are holding onto. There are no compulsions or fixations that we project onto the environment, creating delusional perceptions. We relax and allow what is to be, without judgment or comparison. Because there are no fixations, we are free to flow with the boundless universal energy. This opens us up, lets us be present in the moment, and gives us the opportunity to experience endless possibilities. Being present in the moment allows us to interact with other people without judgment, expectations, or attachment to the outcome of events. The universal flow of energy keeps us vitalized. Interacting with people is no longer draining because we interact in the now moment, realizing that others are as blessed as we are.

The fourth insight teaches us that we need not resort to stealing additional energy from others. We have at our disposal another source, a divine source of spiritual energy for our ultimate security. —James Redfield, *The Celestine Prophesy*

Understanding – With forgiveness, by allowing truth to arise and reconciling it, we process energy that we cling to, which creates a deeper understanding of self. In this depth, we understand other people. Knowing ourselves smashes our fixed beliefs and we realize that what we cling to are beliefs that imprison us in the boundless universe of all possibilities.

Those who look outwards, dream, but those who look inwards, awaken. —Carl Jung

Generosity and Service – Mother Teresa said, "Service is compassion in action." When we understand ourselves, we give to others—we are open, warm, and understanding. We are generous with our time and serve others as we serve ourselves. There is an old Buddhist saying, "None of us gets out of here until we all do." If this is true, then part of our purpose of being here is to help others, because in that service we help ourselves evolve. We should help others only when they ask for help; otherwise we must assume that they are simply following the path that is appropriate for them. During this time we must love them unconditionally. When our assistance is requested, we must serve others as we have served ourselves.

Courage – Ego creates fear—its natural state prevents us from realizing unity and keeps us thinking that we are separate from Source. Self-actualized people have the courage to see truth and do something about it. It is not enough to know it; we need to act on it. If we want to experience true freedom and walk along our paths, we need to take the steps. The universe takes care of us. God feeds the birds, but the birds must come out of the nest to be fed. This is courage. When it seems as though the entire world is crashing down around us and people are acting crazy with malicious intentions, we need to stand up, stay centered, and follow our dreams. This takes courage. Courage is heart-centered and surrounded by love. It helps us realize our true potential of who we really are.

Even if I knew that tomorrow the world would go to pieces, I would still plant my apple tree. —Martin Luther

Gratitude – Many of us focus on what we do not have—we dwell on it. Some of us wish we were someone else, thinking life would be better if we were. Other people do things for us and we take them for granted. Every one of us has a gift, and that gift is the manifestation of who we are. God does not make mistakes. If we were someone else, we would not be able to present the gift of ourselves to the rest of the world. Judy Garland said, "Always be a first-rate version of yourself, instead of a second-rate version of somebody else." When people help us, we graciously acknowledge their unique gifts of self. We are grateful for the ability to experience the wonderment and beauty of the universe from our perspective. Each one of our perspectives is unique and special.

I resent the creation of a world in which beauty is a reminder of what we're losing rather than a celebration of what we have. —Ben Elton

Patience – The unfoldment of the universe moves within its physical laws. There is no time but the current moment; life is a succession of moments. The unfoldment is in divine order. When we think we can change it, we become impatient to have what we want *now*, negating natural order. We think we can will something to happen differently and more quickly than it does. Patience is allowing and knowing that things will unfold in the way they are supposed to unfold, without us getting in its way. This will reveal the grandness of the unfoldment, which is more spectacular then we could ever imagine.

The reward for patience is patience. —St. Augustine

Acceptance – When we are concerned with the outcome of situations, we think that events should unfold the way we want them to, and expect them to be different than they are. We do not trust ourselves, as we do not trust the universe to unfold naturally within universal physical laws. When we do not trust ourselves, we do not trust other people. Knowing that all (including ourselves) will be as it should be is acceptance. We are exactly as we are supposed to be in each moment, if we see the truth and are present in the moment. When we accept that truth within ourselves, we can accept that it is true for other people. There are no exceptions: if we trust in the perfection in each moment, we can accept life the way it is.

As long as man has even the slightest wish that anything might be this way or that, the pure light of truth cannot enlighten him. For example, for a man who in his own review of himself has even the most secret wish that his good qualities might prevail, this wish becomes an illusion and will not allow him true self-knowledge. —Rudolf Steiner

Humor – We take ourselves too seriously, thinking that everything we and others do should be a certain way. We are enmeshed in duality (right or wrong). We put judgmental emotional energy into our lives, and become rigid and inflexible. We get stuck into seeing one side of the duality rather than wholeness. Right is not right without wrong. When we see the truth that right and wrong are opposite sides of the same stick, and that there is nothing the universe considers right and wrong, we transform duality. When we realize there is nothing but unity and that everything occurs as it should, we can see the truth in it and allow ourselves to loosen up and have fun. Therein, we find freedom and joy.

The Enneagram and Compassion

Each Enneatype fixates at one point or another. Forgiveness assists us in liberating these fixations and allows our energy to flow freely. Within each Enneatype lies the potential for attaining traits that lead us to become compassion—not only to be compassionate, but also to live it. Compassion lets us open ourselves and evolve along with the natural flow of the universe, and it aligns our energies with the natural flow of universal energy. At this point Enneatypes begin to resemble whole beings, assimilating spiritual traits from all types.

Enneagram Compassion Traits

Type	Lost or Taken Away	Compassion Trait
One	Perfection	Humor
Two	Self-Worth	Understanding
Three	Authenticity	Warmth
Four	Connection	Gratitude
Five	Intelligence	Openness
Six	Faith / Courage	Courage
Seven	Nurturing	Patience
Eight	Innocence	Generosity / Service
Nine	Significance	Acceptance

One: The Perfectionist – Ones are rigid and inflexible, and take life seriously. They want to be "good boys/girls" and in doing so, live by the rules. Ones often make up the rules based on their own ideas of perfection. If they do not make up the rules, they adopt those that meet their expectations. Ones have incessant internal critics that keep them rigid by constantly nagging and judging their thoughts, feelings, and actions. They repress anger and do not want others to see it. Repressed anger transforms into repressed rage that may surface and explode.

After reaching real forgiveness, Ones begin to open and see humor in how they were. They realize that right and wrong are relative and let go of duality, propelling them toward a state of compassion, as they enjoy life. Their bodies become relaxed and more fluid, and their inner critics are silenced.

Two: The Giver – Twos strive to be needed by others, which they feel brings them love. They will alter themselves to meet the expectations of others in order to get attention. When others do not respond to their offers of assistance, Twos become irritated and demanding. The inner drive to be needed is caused by Twos' lack of self-perception. If we cannot understand our motivations, and ourselves how can we understand others? Understanding ourselves allows us to nurture both other people and ourselves.

After reaching real forgiveness, Twos open themselves to their inner needs through self-understanding. This propels them towards a state of compassion, not only for others but also for themselves. They become less animated and move to inner peace.

Three: The Performer – Threes focus on accomplishments, knowing they will be rewarded through their efficiency and drive to become successful. This drive hardens Threes and they turn off their feelings, creating coldness in their lives. Threes think they have to act because if they do not, nothing will happen. Acting without true conscious connection to Source results in a lack of spontaneity and disharmonious energy flow that negates trust and compassion.

After reaching real forgiveness, Threes open themselves to their feelings and align their actions with the universal energy flow, creating spontaneity. Through feeling, they attain genuineness and warmth and become compassion. They become comfortable in their bodies and slow down, enjoying everything they do and viewing it all as a success.

Four: The Romantic – Fours focus on their uniqueness by seeing themselves as different from everyone else. Comparing themselves to others, they see what others have and what they do not have. Feeling that they lack the happiness they see in others, they withdraw into themselves and fantasize about what they could have. They may become sarcastic and caustic for protection.

After reaching forgiveness, Fours realize they are unique, and in that uniqueness are gifts they received from the universe—gifts they can share with the world. They find gratitude for their gifts and experience compassion. Fours come out of their fantasies and enjoy living their gifts. They become more intentional in their bodies.

Five: The Observer – Fives focus on attaining knowledge because they think they do not possess enough knowledge to live comfortably in the world. They think this way because Fives try to make sense of everything by using their intellect. Disconnected from feeling, they cannot comprehend the truths of the universe. No matter how much knowledge Fives have in their heads, they feel it never is enough, so they withdraw to further accumulate knowledge. They have a difficult time dealing with people in the present moment. People seem to drain Fives' energies because Fives try to think through situations that cannot be understood without feeling.

After reaching real forgiveness, Fives realize that no matter how much knowledge they have, they can live in the moment through openness and feeling. Becoming present in the moment, Fives find that universal energy has no limits, and energy depletion no longer occurs. Presence initiates compassion. Fives loosen up, relax, and enjoy living.

Six: The Doubter – Sixes focus on safety and security in the environment and, in doing so, find dangers. This creates fear and constant movement back and forth in an attempt to achieve safety. They tend to take one step forward and one step back, and sometimes it seems as though they are walking around in circles.

After reaching real forgiveness, Sixes find safety and security within. They trust in the universe and believe that God will take care of them. In faith, they move forward courageously and establish compassion. They loosen up and enjoy life.

Seven: The Epicure – Sevens focus on external planning and activities because they are trying to avoid inner realities containing painful experiences. Thinking they can create their own universal unfoldment, Sevens become impatient and are driven to experience more, because excessive amounts of activity will prevent truth from arising. When they realize that their activities do not prevent inner reality from surfacing, they may become critical of others and themselves.

After reaching real forgiveness, Sevens find that universal unfoldment is natural and spontaneous. Everything that occurs does so in the present moment. They learn patience and allow the universal energy to move through them at its own pace. In the present moment, they become compassion. They become less animated and more serious about living, finding depth and acceptance in their experiences.

Eight: The Boss – Eights focus on safety and security in the environment. Experience tells them to expand their energies, repress their feelings, and become intrusive and offensive to keep people (danger) away from them. This causes them to be self-serving and egocentric. People eventually revolt against Eights, which causes them to withdraw and regroup, looking for ways to attack.

After reaching real forgiveness, Eights find integration of feelings and therefore safety. They learn that they can associate with other people and give of themselves in generosity and service, attaining compassion in the present moment. Eights become comfortable in their bodies and pull their energies inward, becoming less intrusive.

Nine: The Mediator – Nines focus on peace and harmony, trying to avoid conflicts at any cost, including shutting themselves down. This strategy creates feelings of worthlessness, so they look for people with whom they can merge their lives. In merging with other people, they think they can give up their responsibilities and leave decisions up to others. When turning themselves off does not quell inner doubts of their self-esteem, they become fearful and paralyzed.

After reaching real forgiveness, Nines find that they are as worthy as anyone else and realize that conflicts are part of natural law. This creates acceptance of self, and in acceptance of self lies acceptance of others. Acceptance propels Nines into the present moment, where they find compassion. Nines become more determined in their bodies.

19 Waking Up from Our Deep Sleep

Enlightenment is your ego's biggest disappointment. —Paramahansa Yogananda

Consciousness is the totality of the All-That-Is. It is the sum of all thoughts, feelings, and actions, as well as all possibilities. Consciousness permeates all things and lies at the core of all existence down to the smallest quantum particles, waves, and light. It includes the formless, or nothingness.

Why do plant-eating mammals avoid poisonous plants? How do birds know how to build architecturally sound nests? How do trees know how deep to root in order to find water? These creatures are not as intelligent as humans. We have managed to complicate our lives to the point of living unhappily. We strive for everything, yet never become anything but the possibility of potentiality. When most people die, their gravestone might as well say, "He/she died with his/her potential intact." We leave this dimension and transition into the next one never knowing what it is like to live in the glory, wonderment, and beauty that surround us: the kingdom of heaven. We may never know who we are, never return to the loving being we were born as, and never breathe in fresh air and enjoy it without fear.

We believe in separation between Source and ourselves. Separation is an illusion of fear and a manifestation of the ego. We compartmentalize and separate everything, looking for the reasons we are not happy. We say, "It is my inner child acting up," or "Oh, that was in my unconscious," or "My body won't let me do that," or "I am too old." As long as we believe we are separate from the universe, we will not live in true consciousness but will remain narcotized, asleep, and detached from reality. We label ourselves and everyone around us. We even label the inner parts of ourselves (the conscious, subconscious, and unconscious) and think they are separate from the whole. These beliefs negate the wonderful, enlightened beings we truly are.

When we sleepwalk and through the motions of our lives not really know what we are doing or who we are, we establish beliefs we use as crutches. Beliefs are thoughts and patterns we adopt that someone else suggested to us. We begin life indoctrinated by family members who pass along to us their biases, prejudices, incomplete histories, and spiritual beliefs. We adopt these as our own relative truths that may be false, but in order to be accepted, we numb ourselves and follow the herd. We feel righteous indignation when someone challenges our beliefs. How could we be mistaken? How could what we believe be wrong? Millions of people believe that Jews, Blacks, Asians, Moslems, Catholics, or Caucasians are inferior. How can they be wrong? It is their beliefs—beliefs created from irrationality, born out of ignorance, and created from illusions of separation that limit and serve our egos.

There was a time when millions of people believed the earth was flat. Because they believed this, did this make it so? We have heard many people argue that what they think or believe is reality. Did the earth then change from being flat to round because the belief was changed? Or was the original belief based in ignorance? When we say that reality depends upon what we believe, isn't it the same as saying reality is based on our perceptions? If our perceptions are skewed, distorted, and unclear, does that make reality distorted and skewed? Or does it mean that our egos have distorted it, making us think that we can really change it? If we look through dirty windows and see the outside world as grimy, does this mean that the outside world is dirty or does it mean we need to clean the windows? Thinking that reality revolves around our beliefs is narcissistic.

Some of us resist belief systems. Others create their own belief systems based on modernization of ideas, but if those ideas are set in ignorance, irrationality, and separation, we will create more false beliefs to serve our egos. Beliefs are limited to available knowledge that we noted in previous chapters, and may be skewed by those who write history.

When we awaken, we enter into the realm of awareness. We start to notice our thoughts, feelings, and actions. We educate ourselves about life and find that what we think manifests into reality as long as those thoughts are congruent with intent and feeling. If there is incongruence, we manifest what we generate as the highest energy. For example, if we think we want to be rich and find that deep inside,

our feelings of opulence are incongruent with our
thoughts, we unconsciously sabotage ourselves and
remain needy, clinging to the hope that someday we
will make it.

Through awareness, we continue to create
through separation. We are the observers or
witnesses of what we experience, and believe that the
observer is separated from the observed. This is not
true—the observer and the observed are one. We are
still separating our thoughts from our bodies and our
feelings, and some of us try to control every one of
them as though we think we really can. We may try
to control our breathing, thinking that breathing is
the key to existence. If we do not breathe, we cannot
exist in this dimension. We may try to control our
thoughts, thinking that if we are not feeling the way
we think we should feel, there is something wrong
with the way we are thinking. We may try to control
our feelings, thinking that we need to change the way
we feel to match the way we think, as if we know how
we should feel. How should we feel when someone
dear to us dies? Regardless of how much we try to
imagine the way we should feel, when that day
arrives, we feel how we feel.

We know many people who are aware of
themselves and observe themselves but are not
conscious of who they really are. Awareness is limited
to separation and beliefs of how we should be. We are
never who we are as long as we are striving to
"become." We can only be. Being takes no effort.

Consciousness is <u>knowing</u>. It is thinking,
feeling, and doing within the flow of universal energy;
it is doing deliberately. In contrast to awareness,

which is observing, consciousness is a state of being one with what we observe: objects, people, tasks, or nothingness. Consciousness is doing mindfully in the present, <u>now</u>. There is no past or future. Consciousness is enlightenment. It is about being, not about observing being.

There is an old Buddhist saying about enlightenment: "Before enlightenment, chop wood and draw water. After enlightenment, chop wood and draw water." This has been modernized to: "After enlightenment, laundry." The point is that enlightenment is centered in the natural way of things. It is simplistic. Every one of us and everything in the universe is enlightened. If we were not, it would imply that we are separate from unity, and in that separation, strive to be enlightened. Bukkyo Dendo Kyokai, in *The Teaching of Buddha*, explains:

> *As long as people desire Enlightenment and grasp at it, it means that delusion is still with them; therefore, those who are following the way to Enlightenment must not grasp at it, and if they reach Enlightenment they must not linger in it.*
>
> *When people attain Enlightenment in this sense, it means that everything is Enlightenment itself as it is; therefore, people should follow the path to Enlightenment until in their thoughts, worldly passions and Enlightenment become identical as they are.*[13]

---

[13] Bukkyo DendoKyokai, *The Teaching of Buddha*, 60.

As long as we strive to be someone else, we can never be who we are. People want to be like Jesus, Buddha, Lao Tzu, Confucius, Mohammed, or Krishna. We can never be like these people; we can only be ourselves. People tell us, "It can't be that simple." Why not? Thinking it cannot be that simple means that we think we are not good enough the way we are and need to strive to be better or like someone else. In each moment, we are part of the perfection of the universe. How can we not be? How can we improve the perfection of the moment? Everything in the universe flows in perfect balance and harmony. We do too, and can enjoy it if we wake up and experience it. It is we who prevent ourselves from realizing this. We are our own worst enemies, thinking or feeling we are not good enough. WE ARE GOOD ENOUGH! There are no exceptions.

Lao Tzu wrote a wise book thousands of years ago called the *Tao Te Ching.* In the version translated by Stephen Mitchell, he writes of simplicity, compassion, and patience:

> *Some say that my teaching is nonsense.*
> *Others call it lofty but impractical.*
> *But to those who have looked inside themselves,*
> *This nonsense makes perfect sense.*
> *And to those who put it into practice,*
> *This loftiness has roots that go deep.*
>
> *I have just three things to teach:*
> *Simplicity, patience, compassion.*

These three are your greatest treasures.
Simple in action and in thoughts,
You return to the source of being.
Patient with both friends and enemies,
You accord with the way things are.
Compassionate toward yourself,
You reconcile all beings in the world.[14]

Changes

If we are to realize consciousness, we must be able to deal effectively with changes. Changes occur whether we like them or not. We can either accept changes or go kicking and screaming, resisting them. Resistance expends too much energy—energy needed to live life in joy and ecstasy. Change is the only constant; things will change when life is going badly and things will change when life is going well. From a universal viewpoint, everything is just the way it is.

Think about where you were twenty years ago. Where did you live? What were your relationships like? What was your job? Has one of these changed? Have two of these changed? Have all of these changed? Are you better off now than you were?

Changes are essential for the continuation of life. If there were no changes, we would not have been born, nor would we die. Life would be boring, and we would not have anything to learn and experience. Twenty years after the Mount St. Helens eruption, there is new growth. Grasses and lupines

---

[14] Lao Tse, Trans. Stephen Mitchell, *Tao Te Ching,* 67.

grow every year and fill in the old blast area. This growth would not have occurred if the eruption had not taken place. The spewing of lava over the valley brought up nutrients from the earth, and the heat germinated seeds that otherwise would not germinate. In the destruction is life, there is renewal.

Everything changes on a micro level in the short run, and nothing changes in the long run. Everything changes at the surface but nothing changes at the core. The universe always remains as one unified field regardless of how it looks on the surface. All is God, was God, and will always be God.

Changes allow us to travel the road towards remembering— remembering who we really are as we return to the Source. In nature, everything returns to its source. Rivers flow to the sea, and the water in the sea evaporates and condenses, and the rain nourishes the earth's flora and flows to the rivers. Our bodies return to the earth and our souls return to God. Eventually the universe returns to God. Since it is all God anyway, there is really no place to return to. We are already there.

One way to transcend change is to look at things in a new and different way. Paradigms aid us in altering our feelings, and a change in feelings allows us to transcend negative energy such as anger. Also, they allow truth to surface. For example, suppose you are on a bus. At the next stop, a father and his three children get on the bus. For the next few minutes, the children run around and create havoc, shouting, screaming, and so forth. You become angry and approach the man.

"Can't you control your children?" you yell.

The man turns to you with tears in his eyes and says, "I'm sorry. We just got back from the hospital. They saw their mother for the last time. She passed away."

We may transcend anger and replace it with compassion when we know the real story. How can we judge others when we cannot walk in their shoes? Paradigms give us the opportunity to change our perceptions and create new thinking and feeling levels. This process allows us to progress into consciousness. In the *Tao Te Ching*, Lao Tzu writes:

> *If you realize that all things change,*
> *There is nothing you will try to hold on to.*
> *If you aren't afraid of dying,*
> *There is nothing you can't achieve.*
>
> *Trying to control the future*
> *Is like trying to take a master carpenter's place.*
> *When you handle the master carpenter's tools,*
> *Chances are that you'll cut your hand.*[15]

Evidence of Enlightenment

As there are symptoms of those who manifest and live through fear (as discussed in Chapter One), there are "symptoms" of those who have recognized their own enlightenment and live in accordance with universal energy. They are self-actualized.

---

[15] Ibid, 74.

Forgiveness: People who recognize their own enlightenment live with real forgiveness. They find energy blockages within themselves, allow truth to arise, experience it for what it really is, and let it go. They live in the traits of forgiveness described in Chapter 17. They live with Perfection, Self-Worth, Authenticity, Connection with the One, Intelligence, Faith, Courage, Nurturing, Innocence, and Significance.

Compassion: Knowing themselves, they manifest all the traits of compassion and therefore become compassion. These traits (described in Chapter 18) are Warmth, Openness, Understanding, Generosity, Service, Courage, Gratitude, Patience, Acceptance, and Humor.

Trust: In deep knowing, we live in basic trust that the universe is oneness, the All-That-Is, imbued with fixed physical laws and held together by love. Trust is embedded in our soul and exists prior to words and concepts; it is beyond these. Trust is of the universe and means that when challenged, we have the courage to jump into the abyss and know that we will be taken care of by the All-That-Is. Trust aids us in adjusting to objective reality, and relaxes within its unfoldment. Trust is unconditional.

Surrender: Resistance to universal energy is futile. It takes more energy to resist natural unfoldment, and this resistance causes blockages and enhances ego development. Surrender is a choice to live within the universal energy movement—just the way it is—and live within the divine plan. It is the tree that bends in the forest that lives to see another day. When we are flexible, we flow along with the energy of the universe. It is easier to go with the flow of the tide than to try to swim upstream. The concept of the path of least resistance, which is natural in the flow of electricity and the flow of rivers, also applies to each of us. How many times have we tried to go in a specific direction and found that path was blocked to us? Some of us may have tried to blast though the resistance, only to later learn we should not have gone there in the first place. When there is resistance, it means we should go in another direction: that with the least resistance. This is surrender and being led by spirit.

Synchronicity: Everything that happens is for a purpose—divine purpose. It is not important that we know what that purpose is. What is important is that we know there is divine purpose. We may never know what our purpose is; it may simply be smiling at someone someday. We may not know that the person may have been planning suicide and our smile prevented it. In divine purpose, there are no coincidences; everything happens for a reason. Aligning our energies with insight opens synchronicity. We begin to listen to our instincts, messages, and dreams.

Balance and Harmony: When we realize personal enlightenment, we alter internal balance. We no longer need to cling to events that cause us to fixate and obsess. Internal energy flows easily, creating a balance of body, mind, and spirit. When we are balanced internally, we cease to look for external means of balance. This brings peace and relaxation because we do not need to strive for balance externally. An old African proverb says, "When there is no enemy within, the enemies outside can't hurt you."

Harmony is living within frequency vibrations aligned with universal energy. When we are in harmony, all life flows easily, beauty and wonderment are respected. When we are out of harmony, we destroy through fixations.

Mindfulness: Living life in the present, we focus on the simplicity of the moment. We notice that everything is the way it is and see the beauty in all, including ourselves. We are fully conscious and perform tasks for the sake of doing them. For example, we brush our teeth and enjoy brushing our teeth. We remain centered in ourselves and in the present experience. There is no guilt from the past and no worry about the future because in the state of enlightenment, there is no past or future. There is only an endless series of now moments, each one perfect and whole just the way it is. In mindfulness, our intent of purpose is vital and helps us remain in this state. Why does it matter what we are doing, as long as our intent manifests through love, forgiveness, and compassion? When we give our time to charities, for example, why are we doing it? Is it for recognition? Is it to be part of a group? Is it because ego told us to do it for personal gain?

Several years ago we knew two people, George and Valerie, who helped a charity, raise funds for homeless children and their mothers. George raised the most money for the charity, and wanted to be sure his name was printed in their brochures and listed in the newspaper. He thought this recognition would enhance his real estate brokerage career. Valerie, however, raised almost as much money as George did, but wanted no recognition. She did not want her name to appear anywhere and insisted that her efforts be listed as anonymous. She thought her gift was in doing something meaningful. Both of these people did exactly the same thing—the only difference was their intent.

People who live mindfully live deliberately in the all-eternal now moment.

Reverence for Life: Conscious people respect all life; they take what they truly need and waste nothing. They do not kill thousands of buffalo for their hides and leave the carcasses to rot under the scorching sun. They do not join in wars, nor do they kill people. They do not cause harm unto anyone, for they respect and value life.

Detachment: In contrast to Enneatype Five, whose withdrawn stance sometimes seems like spiritual detachment, enlightened beings embrace their false selves, embrace their egos, and live in truth. Detachment means to release our grasp on that which we grasp. Paradoxically, it means to embrace without holding onto our fears. There are no natural blockages in the flow of energy. Detachment simply means to allow ourselves to experience the energy flow in each moment by being present. Kyokai, in *The Teaching of Buddha,* says, "Attachment to an ego-personality leads people into delusions, but faith in their Buddha-nature leads them into enlightenment."[16]

When we are detached, it paradoxically means we live in unity, in the oneness. It does not mean that we try to separate ourselves from experiencing in the moment. Detachment is deeper. It implies not only letting go of ego through experiencing truth, but also letting go of outcomes, desires, and expectations, with the knowing that we will be taken care of. Attachment to these things is the cause of suffering

The *Bhagavad Gita* says:

> *"The wise yogi detaches his consciousness from transitory relationships and possessions, even if living the life of a householder; for he knows all things belong to God, and that at any moment he can be dispossessed of them by divine will. He loves not his family any less, nor does he neglect his duty to them, but rather loves and serves the God in them and expands that caring to include all others of God's children."*

Humility: When we live with knowledge of the unity and oneness of the All-That-Is, we understand

---

[16] Bukkyo Dendo Kyokai, *The Teaching of Buddha,* 77.

that we are no better or worse than others. We are who we are, and manifest the gifts of creation in every cell in our bodies, every thought in our minds, and every feeling in our hearts. In humility, we know we do not advance the evolution of humanity or ourselves by putting down other people. We know we do not advance ourselves or the evolution of humanity by putting down ourselves and withdrawing from living life to its fullest. We know that to serve, we must be served. To give, we must receive. To lead, we must follow. To teach, we must learn.

The Enneagram and Enlightenment

Now that we have detached and let go of our fixations, attained real forgiveness, and live compassion, we live in truth—real truth, not that which is demanded by ego, but the truth that is whispered inside by the soft, loving voice in each of us. The energy flow of the universe moves through each of us, serving up beauty and wonderment in everyday life. The energy flow at this level in the Enneagram is constant. It does not matter whether the flow of universal energy is in the direction of integration or disintegration, because living the highest truths requires no specific direction except in truth itself. There is no integration or disintegration. It is what it is, God manifesting through each one of us.

At the center of the Enneagram at the level of enlightenment is the I AM presence. It is self-actualization. It is acknowledgment of the unity of all existence and nonexistence. It is who we truly are.

As we move into the new millennium, many of us are asking, "WHAT'S THE POINT?" We recognize the patterns we keep repeating—patterns that continue to make us unhappy—and are looking for a way out of this self-destructive loop.

The Enneagram is a good tool for transformation because it depicts probabilities of function and dysfunction of spirit, personality, and ego. It assists us in recognizing ourselves and gives us the ability to transform dysfunctional behaviors into living the truth of who we really are. It achieves this by allowing truth to surface, experiencing it for what it really is, reconciling it, and transforming ourselves into joyful, happy, and content beings living a balance between spirituality and humanity. The Enneagram offers a tool for true self–actualization, the highest level attainable.

Bibliography

Almaas, A.H. *Facets of Unity*. Berekley: Diamond Books, 1998.

Bagdikian, Ben H. *Media Monopoly, The, Fifth Edition*. Boston: Beacon Press, 1997.

Banville, Thomas G. *How to Listen - How to be Heard*. Chicago: Nelson-Hall, 1978.

Braden, Gregg. *Walking Between the Worlds: The Science of Compassion*. Bellevue, WA: Radio Bookstore Press, 1997.

Capra, Fritjof. *Tao of Physics, The*. Second Edition. Boston: New Science Library, 1985.

_____. *Web of Life, The*. New York: Anchor Books, Doubleday, 1996.

Collins, Jonathan. *The Coffee House*. Boston: Element, 2000.

Collins, W. Andrew, and Megan R. Gunnar. "Social and Personality Development." Edited by Mark R. Rosenzweig and Lyman W. Porter. Vol. 41, *Annual Review of Psychology*. Palo Alto, CA: Annual Reviews, Inc., 1990, 387-416.

Condon, Thomas. Enneagram Movie & Video Guide: How to See Personality Styles in the Movies.

Portland, OR: Second Ed. Metamorphous Press. 1999.

Darling, David Ph.D. *Equations of Eternity.* New York: Hyperion Press, 1993.

Dyer, Dr. Wayne W. *Real Magic.* New York: HarperCollins, 1992.

_____. *Your Sacred Self,* New York: HarperCollins, 1995.

Ebel, D. M. "Bar Programs - Other Ways to Resolve Disputes." *Litigation.* 6, (1980)" 25-28.

Elkind, David. "How Teens Handle Divorce." *Parents,* February, 1992, 171.

Garrett, Major. and Timothy J. Penny. *The 15 Biggest Lies in Politics,* New York: St. Martin's Griffin, 1998.

Girdner, L. "Adjudication and Mediation: A Comparison of Custody Decision-Making Processes Involving Third Parties. *Journal of Divorce.* 9, (1985): 33-47.

Hartmann, Thom. *The Last Hours of Ancient Sunlight.* Northfield, Vermont: Mythical Books, 1998.

Hazan, Cindy and Phillip Shaver. "Romantic Love Conceptualized as an Attachment Process." *Journal of Personality and Social Psychology.* Vol. 52, 3, (1987): 511-524.

Hurley, Kathy and Theodore Donson. Discover Your Soul Potential: Using the Enneagram to Awaken Spiritual Vitality. Lakewood, CO: WindWalker Press, June 2000.

_____. *Enneagram for the 21st Century.* Lakewood, CO: WindWalker Press, 2000.

Kyokai, Bukkyo Dendo. *The Teaching of Buddha.* Tokyo: Toppan Printing Co. (S) Pte. Ltd. 1966.

Lao Tse. *Tao Te Ching.* Stephen Mitchell, Translator. New York: Harper Perennial, 1988.

Loewen, James W. *Lies My Teacher Told Me.* New York: Touchstone, 1996.

Maitri, Sandra. Spiritual Dimension of the Enneagram: Nine Faces of the Soul. New York: Jeremy P. Tarcher / Putnam. 2000.

Naranjo, Claudio, M.D. *Character and Neurosis.* Nevada City, CA: Gateways/Idhhb, Inc. 1996.

Nirenberg, Jesse S. *Getting Through to People.* Englewood Cliffs, NJ: Prentice-Hall, Inc. 1963; Reward Classics, 1988.

P'Taah. Channeled by Jani King. *The Gift.* Scottsdale, AZ: 1995.

Palmer, Helen. *The Enneagram.* San Francisco: Harper San Francisco: 1988.

_____. *The Enneagram in Love & Work.* San Francisco: Harper San Francisco, 1995.

Phillips, Peter. and Project Censored. *Censored 1999, The News that Didn't Make the News.* New York: Seven Stories Press, 1999.

Redfield, James. The Celestine Prophecy: A Pocket Guide to the Nine Insights. New York: Warner Treasures, 1996.

Riso, Don Richard. *Discovering Your Personality Type.* New York: Houghton Mifflin Company, 1995.

Riso, Don Richard and Russ Hudson. *The Wisdom of the Enneagram.* New York: Bantam Books, 1999.

Salkind, Neil J. *Exploring Research.* New York: Macmillan Publishing Company, 1991.

Spence, Gerry, *Give Me Liberty.* New York: St. Martin's Press, 1998.

Tipping, Colin C. *Radical Forgiveness.* Atlanta: GOLDENeigh Publishers, 1997.

Trungpa, Chögyam. *Cutting Through Spiritual Materialism.* Boston: Shambhala, 1987.

_____. *The Myth of Freedom.* Boston: Shambhala, 1976.

_____. *Shambhala, The Sacred Path of the Warrior.* Boston: Shambhala Publications, Inc. 1984.

Van Praagh, James. *Talking to Heaven.* New York: Penguin Putnam Inc. 1997.

Wolf, Fred Alan. *The Eagle's Quest.* New York: A Touchstone Book, 1991.

Zukav, Gary. *The Dancing Wu Li Masters.* New York: Bantam Books, 1989.

_____. *The Seat of the Soul,* New York: A Fireside Book, 1990.

Glossary

AKA – acronym for "also known as."

Anhedonia – an inability to experience pleasure. Someone in anhedonic depression will see the world as flat – drained of color and excitement. It is a strategy used to prevent one from feeling. Enneatype Nines experience this to prevent them from feeling the ups and downs in the world.

Assertives – *Hornevian Group* that includes *Enneatypes* One, Three, and Eight. They are expansive, tend to move against people and the environment, inflate the ego, and direct energy outward. Also may be called "people of fire."

Avarice – excessive or insatiable desire for wealth or gain; greed.

Basic Need – Internal, unconscious ego drive needed as a substitute for the false core belief of the loss of connection to Source (Love). We define it as "me".

Bhagavad Gita – a poem of Indian origin about a battle between a prince and his own family; a guide to attaining wisdom and freedom. Considered one of the greatest spiritual books of all time, it has been the inspiration for a great number of other works of philosophy, literature, and art.

Caricature – a deliberate distortion or exaggeration of features and mannerisms of people to achieve a satirical effect. In the Enneagram it is used to depict those people who fit within an Enneatype who display behavior qualities associated with textbook versions of its Enneatype.

Chakras – derived from the Sanskrit term for "wheel"; energy centers associated with major organ systems in the human body; circular vortices where energy is received, transformed, and distributed. The seven most accepted Chakras are at the base of the spine, the lower abdomen below the navel, the solar plexus, the heart, the throat, between the eyebrows, and at the top of the head.

Compliants – *Hornevian Group* that includes *Enneatypes* Two, Six, and Seven. They move toward people, want to be of service, and tend to give in to others to obtain love. Also may be called "people of water."

Ego – the part of the personality that is responsible for the survival of the body. It is what prevents us from running in front of trains.

Enneagram – a symbol made up of a circle that contains a triangle and a hexad (a geometric figure that symbolizes the Law of Seven, which relates to process and development over time). The *Enneagram* symbol is associated with a system of psychological and spiritual growth that is based on nine personality types.

Enneatype – one of the nine basic *Enneagram* personality types.

Epicure – a person who is devoted to sensual pleasure; one with discriminating tastes.

Erudite – possessing extensive knowledge acquired from chiefly from books.

Feeling Triad – the heart-based *Triad of the Enneagram*, which includes *Enneatypes* Two, Three, and Four.

Fixation – stereotyped behavior (as in response to frustration); an excessive or unhealthy preoccupation or attachment. Fixations of the Enneagram occur when as the ego develops and takes over control of the personality.

Gurdjieff, George Ivanovich – a Russian philosopher (1877?-1949) who brought to the West a comprehensive model of esoteric knowledge and founded a school embodying a specific methodology for the development of consciousness.

Heart Point – the *Enneatype* that a particular type moves to when feeling relaxed and secure, with low stress. (For example, a relaxed and secure *Enneatype* One will display healthy behaviors associated with *Enneatype* Seven.)

Hornevian Groups – Assertives, Compliants, and Withdrawns

Horney, Karen – a German-American psychiatrist (1885-1952) who developed a groundbreaking theory regarding neurosis—that it is a way of "interpersonal control and coping." She identified three broad coping strategies: assertiveness, compliance, and withdrawal.

Indolence – inclination to laziness; sloth.

Instinctual Triad – the body-based *Triad of the Enneagram*, which includes *Enneatypes* Eight, Nine, and One.

Introjection – incorporation of external ideas and attitudes into one's own personality. Enneatype Fours use Introjection as a defense mechanism.

Knieval, Evel – a daredevil motorcyclist who was popular in the 1970s.

Mandala – a graphic and often symbolic pattern, usually in the form of a circle divided into separate sections or bearing a multiple projection of an image; a graphic symbol of the universe.

Motto – a maxim of a principle of behavior. In the Enneagram Mottos are used to depict what an Enneatype's typical phrase might be.

Passions – emotional charges that are filtered through egoic fixations. They are obsessive, compulsive, and unconscious. Passions arise as automatic responses to denial of acceptance in the way things are. Examples of passions used by Enneatypes are: resentment, flattery, deceit, melancholy, stinginess, cowardice, planning, vengeance, and sloth.

Path of Disintegration – moving to the *Stress Point*: the pattern adopted by each *Enneatype* during times of extreme stress, when the defense mechanisms associated with the basic *Enneatype* are no longer working. This is the area that presents real growth potential.

Path of Integration – moving to the *Heart Point*: the pattern adopted by each *Enneatype* during times of relaxation and low stress, when they no longer need the defense mechanisms associated with the basic Enneatype. People who are truly here, exhibit evolved characteristic behaviors.

Projected Mirrors – Enneatypes have fixated on issues that prevent us from manifesting our true natures. At some point we give away who we truly are and develop fixations. What was lost or given away create reactions of what is reflected back to us that triggers the repressed feelings of the perceived emptiness. The repressed feeling of loss is projected outwardly onto the environment and is then reflected back to us. We see these as judgments.

Reiki – named after the Japanese word for "eternal life"; a healing modality in which the practitioner transmits energy to another person by holding his or her hands in specific positions slightly above (or lightly touching) the body.

Self-actualization – to fully realize one's potential.

Speech Patterns – Basic Enneatype mode of voice communication.

Tao Te Ching – "The Book of the Way," a classic manual on the art of living, written by Chinese master Lao-Tzu.

Thinking Triad – the mind-based *Triad of the Enneagram*, which includes *Enneatypes* Five, Six, and Seven.

Triads of the Enneagram – the three triads are *Instinctual*, *Feeling*, and *Thinking*. Each represents an area the ego has identified with, which may be the area that is most distorted in functioning.

Type A – a personality that is strict, rigid, perfectionistic, achievement-oriented, and extremely time-conscious.

Security Point – when an average evolved level *Enneatype* attempts to mimic the behavior of their *Enneatype* at the *Heart Point*.

Stress Point – the *Enneatype* that a particular type moves to when under extreme stress. (For example, an *Enneatype* Two under stress will display unhealthy behaviors associated with *Enneatype* Eight.)

Sufi – the term has Arabic origins and is traditionally associated with Islam; a well-known branch of the Sufis were the whirling dervishes of central Asia. Sufis conduct their spiritual life within practical and disciplined activities such as precision movement (dance), allegorical writing, science, alchemy, and music.

Wing Subtypes – the *Enneatypes* adjacent to each type (for example, the Wing subtypes for *Enneatype* Six are the Five and Seven).

Withdrawns – *Hornevian Group* that includes *Enneatypes* Four, Five, and Nine. They move away from people and the environment to their inner world, which seems safer. Also may be called "people of ice."

Worse Fear – internal, unconscious ego drive that we move away from. We define this as "not me".

About the Authors

Justin E. Tomasino Jr., Ph.D. – is a secondary school teacher in Colorado. He is a lifetime member of the International Society of Counselors and Therapists, a professional member of the International Enneagram Association, a certified Hypnotherapist, and a registered psychotherapist. Dr. Tomasino has been studying psychology for twenty seven years and the Enneagram for eleven years.

Inga W. Tomasino – is a Reflexology Practitioner and a Reiki Practitioner. She is a professional member of the International Enneagram Association and a member of the Self-Realization Fellowship. Ms. Tomasino has been studying the Enneagram for five years.